RIEN NE VA PLUS

RIEN NE VA PLUS
ONE LIFE'S COINCIDENCES

Georg Aeberhard

*Von [?]
an Dani
24. 8. '17*

DISTINCT PRESS

Rien Ne Va Plus
One Life's Coincidences
Copyright © 2017 Georg Aeberhard

Summary: *Rien Ne Va Plus* is a collection of individual coincidences which are lined up in chronological order but may be read by themselves. The stories reach from Prague to San Francisco; they are biographical, each one telling of a unique occurrence, sometimes short as an anecdote, sometimes a full story several pages long.

Library of Congress Cataloging-in-Publication Data
2017940325

1. Georg Aeberhard, 1949- 2. Czech Republic - Prague - Biography. 3. Memoirs 4. Short Stories I. Title

Aeberhard, Georg 1949 -
Rien Ne Va Plus: One Life's Coincidences

ISBN: 978-1-943103-06-5

Printed in the United States of America
10 9 8 7 6 5 4 3 2 1

—

DISTINCT PRESS PUBLISHING

If you are interested in bulk ordering of paperback versions of this book, or professional review copies of this book because you intend to write a review in your publication, mention this book on your radio show or podcast, post to your blog or website, or request an article or interview, send your request to please contact us directly at sayhi@distinctpress.com

For more information visit
www.DistinctPress.com

CONTENTS

THE UNBEARABLE LIGHTNESS OF FORTUITY
38th Pocket, The American One

Foreword

What do scientists make of coincidences? I'm sure most have some clever hypothesis to explain them away as random probabilities, but I prefer the theory of Deepak Chopra in *Spontaneous Fulfillment of Desire: The Essence of Harnessing the Power of Coincidence.* Here he says, "When you live your life with an appreciation of coincidences and their meanings, you connect with the underlying field of infinite possibilities. This is when the magic begins."

Yes, the magic! I had recently read and adopted the above theory before I connected with the author of this book, a man who would write lines like, "That's how sometimes it goes: from one coincidence to another, each coincidence opening a door to yet another activity, or a meeting with a new personality."

Yes, it would be one such monumental coincidence which would bring us together... In October of 2010 I was writing a biography I'd been trying to complete for nearly a decade. I was exhausted and I mentioned to a friend that when I finished the book I would take an extended trip to Latin America. My friend raised his eyebrows at this news and said, "Honey, how is this supposed to all work out? You're already broke and now we're adding Latin America into the mix?"

"I don't know...but somehow I'll manage it."

The following week I went to my mailbox and discovered a small package wrapped in brown paper, made even more curious by the exotic allure of foreign stamps. Inside was a letter inviting me to come to Brazil for an extended stay to research and write the story of a woman with the rather remarkable pedigree of having been a political dissident, maid, refugee, television game show personality, cargo boat cook, exotic dancer, laundress, factory worker, jewelry maker, shepherd, trafficker of leftist guerrillas, fashion model, dishwasher, La Scala Opera slave, restaurateur, chorus girl, innkeeper, and Michael Jackson impersonator. Who could resist this assignment?

The author of this invitation was Georg Aeberhard, and through a bevy of coincidences, we would become acquainted when I accepted his assignment. And Georg has now asked me to write the foreword to *Rien Ne Va Plus*, his book on life's little coincidences. But this request, I think, is not a coincidence.

Cathleen Miller is the author of the international bestseller *Desert Flower* and *Champion of Choice*. Currently Cathy's at work on a new book, *On the Run from Rio*.

Author's Note

"My subject: how to explain to you that I don't belong to English though I belong nowhere else."
                    - Gustavo Pérez Firmat, *Bilingual Blues*

Rien Ne Va plus – why this title? What does the title mean? The game is quasi over, having bet and set, win or lose, a life is filling up, no more adventures, no more goals, expectations stilled, no more exploring; curiosity low, the body and mind ready to part – "Rien Ne Va plus"!, the 38 pockets all filled up with one's life's coincidences. In the beginning, an email came in from a highly-respected person: "... *you are yourself quite a good storyteller, you know.*"

Those words have given me the courage to put down these determining coincidences and share them with you, in English, though my mother tongue is Czech and my everyday language is German.

I do thank all the persons (and one animal) who play part in this presumptuous attempt to get even with one's own fate, to my mother and father, to all the L.s, M.s and A.s, alive or dead, in the sense of legacy for their participation in my life - to them all this book is dedicated.

My sincere thanks also go to the publishers, the ladies at DistinctPress in St.Petersburg, Florida, upon whose submission call I reacted, and whose support in the end resulted in this book.

                                        Georg Aeberhard

P.S. There are two types of roulette: the European one and the American one. The American one has one more pocket, with a total of 38 pockets. To me, this 38th one is the most precious.

RIEN NE VA PLUS
Pockets 1 Through 37

Prologue

Do you like the conditional *"if"*? Do you like to imagine a different occurrence of events, to lay out another possible course of a society, of a country, of one's own life? Can you imagine what it might have been like if and when...

...if there had not been the Great War, the Germans would not have secured Lenin's return to Russia in a sealed train carriage providing him with sufficient financial means to start the Revolution in St.Petersburg in November of 1917.

If the Revolution had not been successful, there might not have been the deadly concurrence between the communists and the social-democrats who then have been annihilated wherever possible (Russia, Germany, Spain and later on in all the Middle and the Eastern European countries). The communists were so occupied by fighting the social-democrats that they missed the rise of the national-socialists, the Nazis.

If there had not been the ideological divergence between the bolsheviki (the future commies) and the mensheviki (the future social-democrats), Hitler's regime would not have been able to take over Germany in 1933.

If the Nazis had not been allowed to gain power, there would not have been a reason to start World War Two in 1939. There would not have been any genocide, any terror, no forceful migration...

If all that had not been, the Russians could not have occupied the Middle and the Eastern European countries and - I would not have been born...

...because my father would not have lost his Jewish wife, he would not be a handsome widower who used to walk with his little daughter along the same street as my future mother used to go to and from her work...

"I was born in 1949, entered high school in 1961 and the university in 1967. ... So there I was, during the most vulnerable, most immature, and yet most precious period of life, breathing in everything about this live-for-the-moment decade, high on the wildness of it all..." - thus starts Haruki Murakami his short story *A Folklore For My Generation: A Prehistory Of Late-Stage Capitalism*. He goes on: "I'm not boasting about the times I lived through. I'm simply trying to convey what it felt like to live through that age, and the fact that there really was something special about it. Yet if I were to try to unpack those times and point out something in particular that was exceptional, I don't know if I could. What I'd come up with if I did such a dissection would be these: the momentum and the energy of the times, the tremendous spark of promise. ..."

So there I was born in the same year 1949, born to a life certainly based on no ifs or whens, born to live a life worth living thanks to the "the tremendous spark of promise" in spite of the tragic changes in the heart of Europe, Prague. Where is any coincidence? Where is the stroke of fortuity? It is just the year 1949 which I share with Haruki Murakami, Martin Amis and certainly many more men and women.

2

A Street In Prague

My father Josef married his first wife Elisabeth in 1937 and a year later Alžběta was born, my sister to be. In 1938, the Czechoslovakian Republic was to hand over its border regions to Hitler's Germany. In March 1939, the "Resttschechei" (As Hitler used to call it.) was occupied by German troops and declared "Protektorat Böhmen und Mähren". The Slovaks split, their region became an independent fascist state.

My father's wife was of Jewish origins and when the Germans started to organize the transports, the people of Jewish origins hoped not to be deported because their families had already converted to the Catholic Church, a hundred or more years ago. But the ideology of "Die End-lösung", the "Final Solution", didn't consider such trivia; still there was a minor loophole which excluded a female Jewish person from the ongoing genocide, if married to an Aryan. Thus, my father's wife was safe - so far. But other members of her family were sent to Theresienstadt and farther on to Auschwitz and that caused her unbearable pain. In the end, she herself turned the gas on in the oven at her home in Prague in 1944, committing suicide. She could not bear to lose her father, her mother, her sister...

My father went to German schools in Prague, he knew better German than Czech, and he tried to deal with the authorities. He provided the documents which might exempt the family members from the transports but to no avail.

Since 1941, a young girl was coming and going by the house where my father lived. She did her apprenticeship as a seamstress in the neighboring house and he certainly must have spotted her. Later on, they started to greet each other, and after the tragic death of his wife, my mother's attention to him grew even stronger, seeing him take his little daughter for a walk by himself. In 1945, at the end of World War II, he was 36 years old, my mother 19. My father was lucky to have won her heart because during the critical days of the Prague Uprising she was already staying at his place and when some revolutionary hot heads came to fetch my father because it was known that he kept speaking German, she managed to protect him, not letting them into the apartment while my father was shaking in terror seeing himself already being lynched in the street. They stayed together for life. My mother also became mother to his daughter, and in 1949 she gave birth to me. If it wouldn't be for...

The Savage Eye

La Nouvelle Vague, The Young British Cinema, The Polish and The Czech Wave... But what ignited me to wish to
make films was the American Film *The Savage Eye*.[1] Maybe
I was disposed for it because of Jack London, John Steinbeck, Ernest Hemingway, Upton Sinclair, Sinclair Lewis
or William Saroyan... I happened to see the film *The Savage
Eye* in a press screening in the AM hours, meaning - looking back now - that I had to miss some classes to be able
to do so.

The film's summary by Fiona Kelleghan on IMDb goes
like this: "This drama takes the form of a story told using
documentary material as an intrinsic part of the narrative.
In this journey through the dark side of 1950s urban life,
the camera follows Judith - a newly divorced woman looking for a fresh start - through the streets of Los Angeles as
she encounters the strange denizens of the city, ranging
from trendsetters to religious fanatics. All the tawdry and
desperate faces of this world become a mirror for Judith's
personal failures and struggles to claim her new life."

Now, you really might pose the question what's so interesting about this plot for a 16-year-old in a "socialist coun-

----

1 *The Savage Eye* is a 1959 "dramatized documentary" film that super-
poses a dramatic narration of the life of a divorced woman with documentary camera footage of an unspecified 1950s city. The film was
written, produced, directed, and edited by Ben Maddow, Sidney Mey-
ers, and Joseph Strick, who did the work over several years on their
weekends. *The Savage Eye* is often considered to be part of the cinema
verité movement of the 1950s and 60s

try" behind the Iron Curtain. I remember two things: the black-and-white imagery of the camera work of Haskell Wexler, Jack Couffer and Helen Levitt, its "cinema verité" quality, and my feelings of compassion and empathy with the main female character. I cannot explain why but this theme has become a lifelong obsession with me. I have never been able to make a feature length film but I have several scripts ready in the drawer which deal with the same subject: a woman overcoming "personal failures" and struggling for a new beginning.

At least I was lucky to be able to shoot two documentaries displaying the feminine fight for decency and recognition: the biography of Marianne Werefkin, the Russian painter, friend and mentor of Alexej Jawlensky and Vassily Kandinsky, and the life story of an indigenous Peruvian girl growing up and making life on the outskirts of Lima, in the "pueblo joven" Villa San Salvador, called *Against the Odds*.

Two Adolescent Coincidences

I remember a chance meeting with a girl while waiting for a bus after a track and field regional competition which I won because I have dedicated my last shot put to her, to Helena, an unhappy love of mine. There is a huge area next to the sporting stadium Strahov in Prague. The vast place was used to have sportsmen march up before entering the stadium itself. Now it was empty. A few hours ago, I won the shot-put competition by the last try, thinking of her, dedicating this last put to her, to H. And now she was crossing this place similar to the ill famous Tiananmen Square where I was sitting on the bus stop railing. The summer heat let the air shimmer above the concrete surface. Out of the corner of my eye I saw her silhouette appear, she came closer, glanced at me - passing by, coming to a halt, just to say:

"What are you doing here?"

"What are YOU doing here?"

She kept going and I was gaping after her, totally incapable to tell her anything at all, not to mention to capture her attention...

About a year later, the situation changed; we became kind of friends, she lived through some disillusion, and I was going out with some other girl... Yet we kept meeting and seeing each other not only at school, and the possibility that the two of us might eventually become more than friends hovered above us. We had a date in downtown Prague, but she didn't show up, not for the first time either.

I got really mad and caught a tram to her place.

No one was home. I left a message, venting my frustration, saying something like "I'm fed up, that's enough, I won't ever see you again..." After returning downtown and joining some friends for a beer or two in our favorite pub, I set off home at about an hour before midnight. I got off the tram, and lost in gloomy thoughts I walked towards our apartment building. The street was empty, the yellowish light of the lanterns barely reaching the pavement. Suddenly the night silence of the even otherwise quiet street was punctured by a very special sound, the sound of clicking heels. Judging by the lightness and rhythm of the clicking, a young woman was heading towards me. I raised my eyes from the ground, and with much curiosity looked up at the approaching person. Yes, it was Helena! A few steps later we stopped in front of each other and started to talk both at the same time once again:

"What are you doing here?"

"What are YOU doing here?"

She was relieved to see me; she started to apologize and to explain. Something had happened, she could not make it in the afternoon, and feeling really miserable after she had read my note, she set off across the whole city to save the situation. I don't remember if we hugged at this moment but I certainly more than willingly accepted Helena's explanation and walked her to the tram stop to get back home.

There is a postscript to this episode. After Helena got into our apartment building, and while upstairs ringing the doorbell at our flat, the front door of the building was locked for the night. When no one answered the door, my parents being apparently away, she was stuck inside the building. She waited downstairs in the hall for someone to come in, or leave. The staircase lights were off. At one point, she heard a couple enter the building and was ready to run out but the man and the woman started immediately hugging and kissing, so she quietly withdrew again, waiting unnoticed some more... Well, there is an end to everything. The very end is that we still keep in touch, even though we haven't seen each other for more than 45 years.

Hospiz zur Heimat

When I arrived in Bern, the capitol of Switzerland, on September 23, 1968, just about a month after the Russian invasion into Czechoslovakia, I was relieved and shocked at the same time. I was relieved because I was at the end of my trip, yes, I was going to join my girlfriend Lucie, her mother and some other relatives and companions who all were associated in some way with a Czech refugee from 1948, the year of Communist putsch, who by now lived somewhere here in Switzerland and was supposed to "help" because "he made it". I was shocked because I realized what emigration was about: The language, the culture, the profession... the color of the house fronts... the color of street cars and buses... the weather... And, and, and... And the language, all the more so because a Swiss dialect was spoken here. To ask about the way to my final destination in Bern, I used my self-taught English rather than the "infinitive German" which I learned while working in the German Democratic Republic as a student, in Frankfurt, the one upon Oder, and which I used at the Swiss consulate in Frankfurt, the one upon Main. So I asked in English for the direction to the Gerechtigkeitsgasse, to the hostel "Hospiz zur Heimat". The Old Town section of Bern has a main street that goes down the peninsula slope towards the river Aare, and is divided into different street sections: the Spitalgasse, the Marktgasse, the Kramgasse, and finally the Gerechtigkeitsgasse, all built with arcades on both sides. Why do I mention all this? Imagine you have left home assuming never to come back, and you are going to ask for asylum while to be quartered in a hostel by the name of "Hospice At Home" on a street called the Justice-Alley.

It was a walking distance, I made it fine. I was welcome, and - I could hug my girlfriend, though under the eyes of the hospice personal there, most of them dressed in nun like garments. Immediately I got acquainted with other Czech and Slovak refugees and was able to have a bed in the same room together with all the other members belonging to Lucie's clan; or rather her mother's clan. After being briefed about all the things I needed to know and how to ask for and to obtain political asylum, Lucie and I started to explore the city of Bern...

...A few days later we came "Home" and I was waved to the reception. There I was told that men and women who were not relatives were not allowed to share the same room. As a not related man I had to move out and go to another housing nearby to which local homeless and needy people went as well. I tried to discuss the matter, to dispute the matter, we were going to get married, me and my fiancé Lucie... No! But after a while the hospice receptionist told me, there was a man quartered alone in a double bed room, and if he would be willing to take me up there, no objection, and I could stay at the "Hospice At Home" farther on. The receptionist talked with respect about this man, he was supposed to be a music professor. But since the professor was not in his room right now, I would have to wait and talk to him first. As hour after hour passed by, the hospice life came to a standstill, finally the town's bells announced midnight. I suggested to the night clerk to wait up in the professor's room rather than in the reception hall, and strangely enough I was allowed to do so.

Up in the room, dead tired, I just fell down fully dressed on the one unused bed and fell asleep. I woke up when I heard a gentle voice say: "Pardon me..." It was two o'clock in the morning. An extremely thin man entered the room, quieting me down, "pardon me, I have to switch the light on, just for a second."

I sat up and stretched out my arm for a handshake with the thin man. "Jiří," he said. "Jirka, Jiří, me too," I answered, "from Prague", I added. "Me too," he said. After I got the professor's consent to share the room with him, we both made ourselves comfortable for the night. But we didn't sleep. We kept talking and talking, we got to know each other's background, our specific situation, dreams and goals as well as favorite books and music. We kept talking until the early morning hours, judging by the light outside... This "other" Jiří" - as we were to be known as in Bern - was almost ten years older than me, and actually not only a music professor but also a teacher of Czech language. As it turned out, he even substituted at my school and we might have met already back in Prague.

Now I consider this coincidence - the same destiny, the same one room, the same name - the most important one in my life. This very coincidence conjured a lifelong friend for me (thank you synchrondestiny!) and a string that created an emigre DNA, my template as far as my professional career goes.

Postscriptum: Finally, we both got kicked out of "Home" and had to spend a few nights in the bunk bed dormitory with all its never ending coughing, spiting, slurping, farting and smelling. And that really made us look for some other place to sleep on our own.

The New York Times

CZECHOSLOVAKIA INVADED BY RUSSIANS AND FOUR OTHER WARSAW PACT FORCES; THEY OPEN FIRE ON CROWDS IN PRAGUE

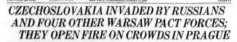

The Secondhand Coincidence

Once you start talking about your coincidences, most people start to offer their own, and so I have started to collect them also. Here are a few which I selected according to their impact upon the lives of the persons they occurred to.

One of the most impressive ones, which has lasted over 40 years now, is the hitch hiking encounter between my Czech friend and her future German husband. My friend is the same age as I am, she also came to Switzerland in 1968 and acquired political asylum here. Her lifelong coincidence happened five years later, when she lived near the border between Switzerland and Germany, at Lake Constance, but studied at the university of Bern, some 150 miles west of her latest temporary home town. One day in the month of May she - let's call her Jitka - had to sit for an exam in Bern, and as a student working her way towards a degree, Jitka relied on hitch-hiking to commute to the university. She held her thumb up on the side of the highway in the direction of Zürich and farther on to Bern.

Jitka was a lanky, blond girl, at 25, a woman at her best, attractive enough to easily secure a ride even for an important exam. A car with a German license plate stopped for her soon enough, and after Jitka assured herself that the driver was heading towards Zürich, she got into the car. The driver, a man alone, greeted Jitka in High German while turning down the volume of his car tape deck. Jitka returned his welcome and said immediately: "Oh, no, please, let it play!" The music which she encouraged to keep listening to was a Moravian song, a song from the very region of her origins. The driver nodded in agreement with Jitka's wish, kept the tape running and inquired eagerly about her excitement over the folk song played by the ensemble "Moravanka". They got to know each other on the spot. On their way to Zurich they chatted, shaking their heads over this "Moravian" coincidence from time to time. The man turned out to be very polite, almost an old style gentleman, a few years older than Jitka, he had an air of a man who was always ready to comply with anything a woman might desire. Already then, while sitting at the wheel, Jitka saw that the man was taller than herself, and she instinctively liked his finely cut face. The man introduced himself as Wolfgang, right then on his way to Zürich to buy himself a new tie.

Before Jitka and Wolfgang separated on the outskirts of Zürich, where she could get another ride towards Bern, the two of them had already exchanged enough information so that a future encounter might have come true anytime thereafter. As a matter of fact, it did happen the very same day or rather night. Jitka managed her hitch-hiking trip to Bern on time, she passed the exam, and in the evening, she was back at Lake Constance so that she could keep her job at a music bar in the town of Constance. Wolfgang did not hesitate to show up. He spent the whole evening there, waiting for her work shift to end. It was a nice warm night, the sky above the lake free of clouds, slightly misty along its coast. Wolfgang took Jitka for a trip all around "his" lake, told her about his empathy for the Slavic countries which went as far as having a subscription for a publicity magazine *In The Heart Of Europe* published in Czechoslovakia in German language. Why all this?... Wolfgang told

16

Jitka that his father died on the Eastern front, somewhere in the Ukraine during WWII, not having ever seen his son. Consequently, as a war orphan Wolfgang was not obliged go into the German military service but instead he served his time with the civil defense.

Close to 4 o'clock in the morning, when Jitka was dead tired, she asked Wolfgang if he would know about some bed for her... Yes, Wolfgang did, and thus this almost 50 years long love affair at first sight begun and has lasted till today.

The Dog That Owned Me

In his bestselling book *The Spontaneous Fulfillment of Desire ('Harnessing the Infinite Power of Coincidence')* Deepak Chopra talks also about nonlocal communication between dogs and men. He mentions the scientist Rupert Sheldrake and his experiments: "From ten minutes to two hours before their owner arrives, the dog will sit at the front door and wait, as if anticipating the owner's return." I had the same experience, though I was not an owner of a dog. It was the other way around.

At the beginning of the seventies, I lived by myself in a village in Switzerland, in a small rented house called Stöckli, a place parents retire to when their children take over the farm. At first I lived in a commune, and there the inhabitants used to keep at least one dog (and quite a few cats). In the village itself, the native dogs were reigned over by a magnificent specimen of the Bernes Sennenhund. Another dog race present in the village was a Black Newfoundlander. At that time, the dogs moved in and around the village with liberty, and thus the Newfoundland bitch was impregnated by the magnificent Bernes male. Their bastards didn't come out as bastards but looking like either a thoroughbred Bernes or thoroughbred Newfoundland race. The Newfoundlander started to live with the people of the commune; the Bernes one, named "Baeru", with a farmer's family about a hundred feet away from my Stöckli. Baeru grew up into a strongly independent character and in spite of the fact that I was not feeding him or trying to keep him at my place in some other way, as soon as I showed up, Baeru was there. The owners chained him but he kept howling continuously, facing the direction of my house. So they gave up on Baeru, and he roamed the village at liberty as his father did.

The communication between him and me, his anticipation of my irregulars returns, is the subject of this one nonlocal synchronicity between a man and an animal. I was working freelance in Zürich, about 70 miles away, and I worked irregular hours. But for more than two years while I was commuting to and from Zürich, any time I arrived at the house, Baeru was there when I parked the car. He was lying on all four in front of the lights of the automobile, his head raised and slightly tilted in anticipation, fully at ease, playfully looking at me. Yes, he owned me, yes, in this case it was the other way around. But it WAS there, between the two of us, the "nonlocal communication".

The Name Jiri (Jiří) = George

As a freelance script writer and director I used to work for the Swiss German Television from time to time. On one occasion, looking at the credits at the end of a half hour documentary on "stress", you might think you have watched a Czech television program judging by the names:

Camera Jiri Hase
Editing Jiri Slavicek
Written and directed by Jiri Havrda

How did this come about? Ask the man at the switchboard from The Swiss German Television... Neither of us Jiris has asked for that kind of clustering.

Another meeting with a man named Jiri happened at the Municipal Theatre of Bern where I was lucky - totally penniless at that moment - to find temporary employment as an operator of a spotlight. The circus like search light follows the main characters of a play or an opera from the upper loges of the auditorium, placed left and right to the stage. I was in the left loge, the other Jiri was in the right one. This compatriot of mine was around forty years old, a single man, and he was one of those people that wished to give the impression they know already what you mean before you might have finished your sentence. Also, secretly, he was in love with beer, even at work... So we went through the rehearsals, even though the special ones just for the two us with the spotlights because there were several moments when we had to take over a character from each other as the actors exchanged their position on the proscenium, and they became unreachable for the originally assigned beam. There were some blunders during the rehearsals but my companion was assuring everyone that he "got it". Well, he did not. So, as the performances started for real, from time to time, a main character which had nothing to sing or recite, stood there overexposed in a double spotlight while the performing one was plunged in darkness, raising a voice in frustration, screaming for attention, so to speak.

As proper divas, the actors ended up in the double light together, sacrificing the rehearsed stage directives for their solos in order to be actually seen. When such a scene ended, yet another confusion took place: the disco like movements of our beams followed the actors for a moment until we rested our lights on each character separately, and we usually improvised in this manner until the play came to an end. Naturally the actors were mad at us, they hated us. Jiri did not last long, neither did I. I have not seen my namesake ever since.

The Zero Hour Coincidence

In the month of December 1980, I found myself back in Zürich after having spent several weeks in Lima, Peru, looking for a subject for a film about children living in poverty. Never before, since I left Prague 12 years previously, did I feel so estranged from reality, the Swiss reality.

The feeling of alienation grew even stronger since there was no one there waiting for me. The imaginary glasses through which I looked at my environment from the very first moment on after landing back in Zürich-Kloten let me see a panel of wealth which I was unable to align with the world of poverty I was returning from.

My depression was complete, down to zero, yet I did not feel any despair. It was just a mental state of total isolation from the passersby, on the verge of heavy melancholy.

On the day of arrival, back inside my four walls, and when I was drunk enough to fall into bed and sleep and sleep and sleep, I realized that the clock on my bedside table had stopped many days, even weeks ago. I grabbed the phone and called the time, the 161 number.

What I got to hear was just the summary of the state of my mind: "Es ist Null-Uhr, Null-Minuten, Null-Sekunden..." I pressed my forehead onto the cool glass of the French window near the phone.

I would not have ever imagined there could be such an announcement as: "The time is: zero hour, zero minute, zero seconds. The time is:..."

An Afterword

The "Neue Zürcher Zeitung" January 8, 1981, ran an article about Lima, Peru, entitled *Lima on its way to become a city of misery*. This article came out a fortnight after I returned from the above-mentioned research trip to the Peruvian capital. The article provided the reader with the following information. Here are just fragments of the basics: "In 1977 already 1.2 million people, (almost a third of the total population of 5 million), were living in approximately 350 "Pueblos Jovenes" of Lima. At the time of writing, only about a half of the households in these settlements have water and power. On top of this, in these quarters there are only few Medical Centers or schools. ... In regard to the income tax; there are only 90 000 tax payers, out of 6.4 million citizens entitled to vote in Peru. ..."

Star Wars at the End of the Road

John Barth wrote his second novel *The End of the Road* in 1958, and in 1970 a revised edition was published and the novel was made into an indie film which is almost forgotten by now. The film was directed by Aram Avakian and had a superb cast: Stacy Keach, Harris Yulin, Dorothy Tristan and - as Doctor D. - James Earl Jones; the story of the book (and the film) briefly: its protagonist, Jacob Horner, suffers from a paralysis called "cosmopsis" - an inability to choose a course of action necessary for life. As part of his therapy, his Doctor has him take a teaching job. Horner befriends the strict gym teacher Joe Morgan and his wife Rennie, with whom he becomes entangled; a tragic ending of the affair follows. Doctor D. tries to save the situation by performing abortion...

The book was recommended to me after I went through similar affair myself, which in my case - fortunately - didn't end in any tragic aftermath. But certainly, the book as well as the film left a deep impression on me, not only thanks to its story, but also thanks to the one character Doctor D. And above all it provided me with a special understanding of the US culture (and subculture!) before being able to make my own experience.

About ten years later I was to record commentary for an English version of a fund raising short film for a worldwide organization, and as a voice we selected the voice of James Earl Jones who previously lent his fabulous vocal organ to the character Darth Vader in *Star Wars*. The collaboration

25

with the great actor turned out perfect, professional and hearty at the same time, full of reciprocal respect and to the best of the attempted result.

I hope this is not considered just name dropping. For me, this row of events on a string based upon the novel by John Barth is quite essential for understanding the American culture and my relation with it, including its representatives, should they be white or black. That's how I also learned to respect the entertainment business in the USA on a personal level. Thank you, Darth Vader, I mean James Earl Jones.

The Impostor's Stroke Of A Chance

July 17, 1979. At about 5 PM I set off for my favorite bar near the river Sihl in Zürich. In front of the place there you could sit outdoors as well, and drink - maybe a glass of white wine. One person was already sitting there, a girl of about 20, beautifully shaped, maybe with a breast too large for her fragile figure, a neck remarkably slender, skin delicately whitish, her hair shoulder length, of a very fair blonde color, eyebrows almost invisible. She reminded me of the actress Rosanne Arquette. When I was sitting down at the table next to her, she smiled gently, nodding in affirmation. The affirmation I could not decipher. I returned her smile, her nodding, assuming that the young lady was enjoying the pleasant summer evening, and was expecting a polite confirmation. Young ladies around here and inside the bar Helvetia were no exception. The bar as well as the outdoor area were quite popular with the girls and women who worked as operators for the Swiss "111", general information phone service. And no wonder Helvetia was thus popular with men as well.

We were sitting watching people hustling home from work. We watched the blue street car lines passing by, screeching in their rails... We started to exchange looks with each other, both keeping a slight touch of a smile around our lips. In the end, it was me, not really knowing how to start a conversation:

"Everyone rushing home... Are you working at 111? Have you finished? Or are you going to work?"

"No, I'm done for today."

Again, we smiled at each other, the girl's eyes being unpretentiously clear, innocent, inviting to keep up the conversation.

"May I?" I asked her and walked over to her table. She nodded and I sat down.

That's how I met Erika. At that moment she was 19-years-old, exactly 10 years younger than me. We kept up our conversation, we felt more than comfortable in each other's company, and in the end we had a dinner together, in the very end we went to my place to drink some wine and to listen to music, in the very, very end we ended up in my bed. While the time of this unexpected happiness was ticking, I got to know Erika and her story. Erika, a tender female, being just 19, was still a rosebud. She was the youngest of five children in a farmer's family from which she ran away. She also had just ended up with a friend who was a drinker, after 8 months of being together. She told me everything without any affect and I felt happy to be able to give her my arms to confide to. In between, we made love and I was sorry to discover that she learned - or better, was taught - certain sexual techniques which I abhorred. Gradually, I brought her back to a level I liked, and she was fast to relearn being soft and simple. We were drunk with each other, thirsty for love, half awake, half sleeping in each other's arms. Shortly before dawn, I woke up. I was crossing the apartment. It had windows into four different directions. In the heat of this summer night I sensed inquietude all around, the city breathed with tension. In the neighboring windows opposite to ours I spotted people moving around like specters. I went back to Erika to hold her tightly in my arms. She was sleeping deeply, rolled together like an embryo. I enwrapped her fragile body kissing her gently on her slender nape. Then I fell asleep again.

In the morning our love was still around, though we knew that this was just one night to share. Erika sat herself on top of me, hitting me playfully on my chest, saying: "You know, you are the wrong one. You are an impostor. There, I've had a blind date... some man I didn't know at all. He called '111' the night before, we started to chat. In the end I've suggested to meet him at 5 PM, in front of the Helvetia Bar ."

"Really?..." I wondered. "And?"

"I've no idea, I've not see anyone else around at that point. Only you."

"But you must have known that I wasn't him. Because of the language at least, no?"

"Yes. But I didn't care anymore. I fell for you..."

I've kept seeing and meeting Erika for a while, she had a new friend, first a real long haired, overaged hippie, then I saw her with a Peruvian man wearing a genuine poncho. Later on, several years later while already living in another country, I happened to run across a newspaper article in the *Tages-Anzeiger*, the Zürich daily. It said that in a spiritual confusion, an Indio refugee from Peru decapitated his female companion E. by a stroke of a machete. E. ... Erika. Erika - why did I have to get a copy with this kind of news when I was not living there anymore? Why did I have to find out and see Erika's gentle nape immediately in front of me? Now forever smeared by the image of her decapitation...

The Lakota Fortuity

While I was co-directing a documentary in The Yellow
Thunder Camp in the Black Hills, South Dakota, I had to
call my production company to demand better equipment
for our New York crew. Back in Europe, my phone was
picked up by someone I didn't know but whose voice had
charmed me so much that I was struck by the urge to fall
in love with the magic woman behind it, her voice deeply
sonorous, yet wide open at the same time, sensuous in its
timbre. For me, the scenery was unreal: to make the phone
call, I had to drive out of the camp, out of the Black Hills.
The first phone booth available was right there where the
Great Plains start to unroll. Three extremely different landscapes come here together. The inhuman Bad Lands, the
lush Black Hills and the windy Great Plains. The voice ten
thousand miles away from this telephone booth, belonged
to a woman who served on the company's switch board
as a temporary summer vacation replacement. The voice
exercised something like a magnetic field rich on intimacy
which - on my part - caused a flow of words I was losing
control of. By the end of our conversation the voice got a
name: Helena. On top of everything the sorceress told me
that she was very much involved in human rights work
for indigenous peoples, especially for the Lakota and other
Native Americans. The coincidence? Do a documentary
on Sioux Indians in South Dakota and meet their advocate
on the phone in Zürich, just by chance.

Retracing this coincidence, I cannot help but to tell the

whole story. First, Helena was a charming person not only "voice-wise" but also in person and we actually became friends. The documentary was pre-edited in New York, the final work being done in Zürich a few months later. The leading personality, thanks to which the filming was made possible and was also based on, was Russel Means, the American Indian Movement leader. The initiative for this film came from his Spanish blood brother Gines Serran Pagan who is ethnologist, painter and sculptor.

Meeting Fools Crow in Prague

When I started to live in the Czech Republic at the end of the nineties, I was sharp to follow the publishing situation there, respectively to track translations from English. I have to say, it was a time of great satisfaction, missing literary parts of the western world culture were filled in quickly, almost too fast. On one occasion, at the book shop window in Prague's Opletalova street, I immediately spotted a book because I knew the cover picture. It was the Czech issue of *Fools Crow* testimony which I have had in English and which carried the very same cover picture. Astonished I shook my head, went inside and acquired the book.

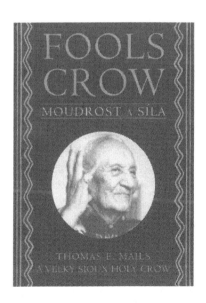

Fools Crow? Here is one of his obituaries:

"Frank Fools Crow, a Sioux Indian spiritual leader who helped to negotiate the end of a 68-day insurrection at Wounded Knee, S.D., in 1973, died Monday at the home of his grandchildren. Mr. Fools Crow, whose exact age was not known, was believed to be 99 years old. He was born near the Wounded Knee Indian Reservation, quitting school in the third grade to work to help his family. As he grew to manhood, he said, he traveled throughout the nation with the Buffalo Bill Cody Wild West show. In 1973, members of the American Indian Movement seized the village of Wounded Knee, S.D., in an armed revolt to protest the Federal Government's policies on Indians. The seizure lasted 68 days, ending after an agreement was reached between Federal officials and a Sioux delegation of which Mr. Fools Crow was a prominent member. Mr. Fools Crow, a medicine man, had lived with grandchildren near Kyle after the death of his second wife, Kate, in October 1988." - AP, Published: November 29, 1989

I met Fools Crow in person in 1985, three years before he died, at his home. Together with Gines Serran Pagan, we did a documentary on yet another land seizure by the American Indian Movement, the seizure of The Yellow Thunder Camp in the Black Hills, South Dakota.

At that time, the prominent leader of the AIM was Russel Means (died October 22, 2012). Since Gines Serran Pagan was a "blood brother" of Russel Means, we were invited to stay in the Yellow Thunder Camp in a teepee set up for the crew, we were even able to film the Sundance Festival (except for the actual initiation rite), and we were introduced to people like Fools Crow. In the film, he told us - here translated into English - that "the Lakota people will never sell their land. One day they will live again in the Black Hills, and they will able to live off the land which the Great Spirit has given them."

The Forgotten Coincidence

Once I remembered a coincidence which I immediately noted down using its future title as a crib: "Black To Black". I liked the title very much so. Unfortunately, in the meantime, I have forgotten what the coincidence was about.

The Resurged Coincidence or "Black to Black"

You remember the "Forgotten Coincidence", don't you? Well, the coincidence came back to me a few days in... Yes, in the bathtub. Thinking things over, I came back to the memory hook "Black to Black", the title I liked so much but have forgotten what the coincidence was about. Such a fancy title must wrap some special content! And I started to go through people, landscapes, occurrences, objects looking for their common denominator "black". Suddenly it clicked: My black car, her black car! And both the same brand. We got to know each other at a bar, I had approached her, we made a date for a Saturday afternoon to go visit my favorite museum, the Oskar Reinhart Collection am Römerholz in Winterthur, which she didn't know about. The date worked out, we stayed together for 18 years. But the startling coincidence in the beginning was created by our cars. She drove a black Fiat Panda, I drove a black Fiat Panda.

The "International Herald Tribune" Coincidence

St. Petersburg, a few years after its name changed from Leningrad. You switch the name of a place but the identity stays with it. We were lodged in the hotel St. Petersburg located directly across from the embarcadero where the ill famous cruiser Aurora was, and still is, moored.

In the hotel, we were to deal with a few things extraordinary for a Westerner, yet for someone of origins from behind the Iron Curtain, they were specifically Soviet like, and, in the end, Russian. At that moment, the hotel could be used only up to the fifth floor (see picture). Above, it was blackened because of a devastating fire which occurred a short time ago. On every floor, there was a "deszurnaya", an overweight, middle aged woman sitting at a small, camping like table in front of the elevator doors but with a free sight left and right into the corridors. She not only controlled "the situation" but could arrange for any kind of service day and night, bringing you a cup of tea, exchanging money privately, organizing a "hostess" and so on. Out of the hotel room window you could admire the slowly flowing river Neva and the buildings aligning her width as well as to watch the navy rituals on and around the historic cruiser Aurora. The hotel's dining room was run strictly according to preset operating hours, creating frustration not only as in regard to one's need for a coffee but also to one's integrity as well. The serving personal might already be there, standing at their posts according to their individual functions but they would not start to move before the - their! - correct set time (which of course was not known to the guests). Should you rebel or try to draw attention, you would be mercilessly reminded of your negligible existence, by a devastating, stern glance.

It was a relief to be out of the depressing hotel, out of the frustrating dining room, out of the impersonal hotel lobby. There I usually grabbed a copy of the *International Herald Tribune*, the only foreign newspaper available. We waited for our transportation which was to bring us, day by day, to different locations interesting for our documentary about Domenico Trezzini, the Swiss Italian architect who - commissioned by Peter the Great himself - laid out the port town on Neva at the Golf of Finland, and supervised its naissance until he died there in 1734. St. Petersburg, this to-be new capital of Russia, was also to become the gate to the West.

Because of the language, on this documentary project I was working together with my usual crew from Prague, whose members knew Russian as well as I did since we all had to learn the language until 1989; from the fifties on, Russian was the first and only mandatory foreign language at school, starting at age ten, and continuing into university studies. Nevertheless, we contracted a Russian production manager who looked after our well-being and also organized the shooting at the numerous locations.

Our mini bus, driven by usually good humored, yet phlegmatic Wassja, had arrived, and while the Russian production manager still had to do some phone calls out of the hotel lobby, we took our seats in the run-down vehicle. I glanced over the front page of the *Herald Tribune*, and then flapped it over to the back side. There a sympathetic woman was facing me, the title introducing her as "The Ambassador for Czech Glass". I had skimmed over the article, and on the spot, I passed the information on to the Czech production manager. "Yes, that might be something," was his reaction, "let's pass the article on to Prague." Yes, we did so. The theme raised some interest with the Czech Television, and the production was launched, though some funds had to be secured first in the West since the "Ambassador" was residing in Hamburg, Germany.

So a year later, in 1995, we found ourselves in Hamburg, to be exact in its suburb Hittfeld where the charming ambassador ran her glass art gallery, exhibiting exclusively Czech glass artists such as Jan Fišar, Milan Hand or Ilja Bílek, prominent artists not only in Europe but in the USA and Japan as well.

That's how sometimes it goes: from one coincidence to another, each coincidence opening a door yet to another activity, or a meeting with a new personality. I have loved these stretches but by 1999 I ran out of luck.

Free Swingers

Switzerland is not a big country, with a population of up to 8 million at most. So if you look for the very same model of an outdated chair to complete your set in a gallery, and you find these so called "free swingers" right across from the place where you need them, it's really a great coincidence, isn't it. How? Using a platform similar to ebay, I set up an ad for black leather free swinger chairs and was contacted immediately by a neighbor across the street who was moving out of his apartment and was happy to get rid of them for a symbolic value right on the spot...

How We Die

"A couple of centuries ago, sixty used to be considered old, and since none of us thought we would live past thirty, reaching the double of that isn't half bad, is it?"
- Paul Auster, *The Invisible*

"'Turning thirty was a surprise,' he said while lifting a brown mug to his lips. 'I never thought I would live to be thirty.' Richard Brautigan to his daughter Ianthe when she was eight years old."
- Ianthe Brautigan, *You Can't Catch Death*

Beginning October 2010 I went through a heavy old age crisis: serious health problems, divorce, looking for a new place to live by myself, etc. Being extremely lucky to find the perfect one room apartment in a quiet street in the Old Town here, I started to pass by a used book store. In front of the store there was an old banana box labeled "For Free". On one occasion a very particular book attracted my attention: *How We Die* by Sherwin B. Nuland. I picked it up and carried it home with me. It's a great book, it helped me a lot.

On another occasion, just around the corner, I ran across a leaflet stuck behind a drainpipe which was announcing a booklet *Suicide - The Best Solution* by someone by the name Philipp Müller, including a link to the web site www.ja-zum-Freitod. If this book is going to help me I won't ever be able to let you know.

A Perverse Coincidence

"...sex divorced itself from feeling. Pornography was the industrialization of that rift..."
                    - Martin Amis, *The Pregnant Widow*, 2010

October 2010. Dear reader, imagine: your marriage falls apart after 20 years, your heart is broken (literally), you have to start to live all by yourself in a provincial town where you ended up only because of the origins of your wife, you have to live in a place where you know nobody, have no friends. Nevertheless, this is the one and only life you have got, and you need love: a new woman to be with; no future wife, no, you only wish not to drown but to keep swimming.

In our age, social media offers unlimited opportunities to get to know all kinds of people, male or female, some normal, some maniacs, some freaks, and lots of perverts. The match making platforms, for a man of your years (50 plus), are a reasonable step to take, you don't want to end up as an alcoholic hanging around bars on the lookout for a chance encounter. So you take your chance here. You design a portrait of a future female companion you would like to meet, you set the possible geographical range of her domicile in regard to your own, marking the age group, adding the status restrictions as alone, separated or divorced, not wishing for someone seeking mere sexual side steps while being married (surprisingly very popular). Yes, I am a conservative person as emotions go, linear so to say. You click the button, the ball is rolling, the search starts - and hits a suggestion which you certainly wouldn't have expected: The first face the match making platform conjured for you is - the face of your own wife, now separated... Looking fresh, perkily provocative, she presents herself under the suggestive surname "Butterfly". You have to look twice, you have to look again and again. You are after someone who might be able to replace the 20 years of your life and the first one to encounter is the one who has just denied those 20 years of living together, making you just a simple cuckold. That's my perverted coincidence.

M. for Meret or The Match Making Chance

After the shock of facing my ex on the screen of the first match making platform, some time had to pass before I launched another attempt to meet a woman virtually. This time I chose a match making site that praised itself for being for the elite, and the fee was set according to the acclaimed level. Though I was no academic, neither teacher nor a professor, neither engineer nor manager nor a CEO, I dared to present myself as an educated, independent and freelancing person. The members of this platform were not going to leave "their love" to a coincidence (sic!) or to go for it "target driven". Money paid in, I profiled myself as attractive in the age group "50-plus" and submitted the text as well as a picture of myself to the virtual levels: "I speak several languages, I know my way around the world, I have no more illusions, yet I believe in purity and affection". Yes, rather sentimental, romantic, but that is what I desired after the unexpected cuckoldry. Also, as important values, I declared freedom and the pleasure to give away, and that it would make me happy to find HER and together enjoy "tenderness and confidence. Chores of music included".

The hours at the lap top, my working instrument, were now loaded with expectations of e-mails offering at least "a smile". Any e-mail announcing itself from the match making platform raised my excitement of a coming date with a person unknown but lovable - with HER. A certain number of ladies expressed their interest; singles, divorced, mothers of grown children, from all kinds of regions. The very first one I was supposed to meet physically, "in specie" so to say, was a music teacher, who immediately passed her telephone number on to me since she was not a paying member and was afraid to miss the opportunity. On one of the coming days I happened to be in the vicinity of her town, and, on a whim, I phoned her and she agreed to meet me in person. Now she was sitting across the table in an anonymous coffee place and we started our conversation surprisingly easy. But the reciprocal presentation turned out to be disappointing in its outcome. This SHE, she was a case for welfare. Everything in her profile was correct, yet was wrong. She was a music teacher but had no job or assignment. She was living on the edge, she was looking for a man but for a man to drag her out of her situation, to show her at least a way out. As she said, she didn't care where she would go, if it might be somewhere in Switzerland or maybe Amsterdam, Prague - that would be OK with her also. No, I was not the man for her, certainly not. Under the pretext that I wanted to drive back home during day light, I quasi-snuck away. Sorry.

The next meeting "in specie" happened - by a coincidence. I started a virtual e-mail conversation with a certain M. who was living in my region. On a Friday evening I went to a jazz concert in my home town, and while I waited in line to get the ticket, I spotted a woman passing by, whose amateurish photograph I saw a few days before in her match making profile. Having paid for the ticket, I proceeded to the bar where M. was waiting to order. I touched her shoulder shyly: "Excuse me, please, aren't you M.?" Yes, just simply "M.", I didn't know her full name. SHE nodded with a smile, "M. for Meret"...

This was the second virtual coincidence after facing my ex on the web on my first go there. Although, let's go back to the beginning of the story of "M.". The woman behind this letter "M." imagined her relation with a man in this way: to be mutually tolerant. To respect each other, to accept each other's freedom without enforcing unnecessarily some "common world" of similar points of views or values. To be mutually attracted. Tenderness and sex being especially important. No less than 30 days had to pass by before I met Meret by chance in person. This is what makes the meeting so special (for me at least). It was a month-long effort which culminated in the unexpected meeting at the jazz concert. I was the one who approached her through the elite platform and she responded, stating psychology as her profession:

"Dear F.
Not only because you are living in Bienne, you have attracted my attention! It's probable that we move in similar circles and we seem to have many common interests.
Cordially M."

"Dear Psychologist
It's a pleasure to respond to you. I only do hope that my ex-wife is not a client of yours... F. stands for Franta, my alias. I would love to see a picture of you, mine is available.
All the best to you, F."

Nothing.

"Good morning, M.
I thought about the possible areas and establishments which you

might be frequenting in our town:
A) the alternative cultural line through the Old Town
B) the modern style fancy parts in the station district..."

Nothing.

"M.
I am asking myself where could you have got lost - on line A or
B? Or is there a C also?"

Nothing. Seven days were gone, M. kept silent. Why? What did I do wrong? Or did not do properly... Almost in despair I wrote to her:

"Am I being refused? I would prefer a clear-cut 'No'. What has
psychology to say to that? I'm wondering, F."

Nothing. Two more days later, the day being Saturday, the day of the market in the Old Town, I wrote to M.:

"OK, if you happen not be curious about me, please, pass a word
to me. Even if the sparks shouldn't fly between the two of us, I'm
glad to get to know someone here in my new home town (after
having lived in Prague, Bern, Zürich, San Francisco). Yours,
F."

We have reached the tenth day of our virtual tour. M. finally answered:

"We might call it dodging, you really are stubborn! A few an-
swers here: I'm frequenting the area 'A', you were right there!
Your wife is not a client of mine because children are my main

field. I was at the market as every Saturday, for sure... And, by the way, I was in San Francisco shortly, for 10 days... Once again, this avoidance... Your profile is quite exciting but I've problems with your pictures. And I'm aware of the fact that I've not uploaded any of mine. So long, M."

So long... This back and forth exchange was to last for almost a whole month. If only I could not be so curious... I really wondered what the rather high score of 94 matching points had been based on... So long or a "Good bye, forever"? In regard to the high score I got a stunning answer:

"As a psychologist, I've to say that the matching points don't have much meaning really. By the way, I'm about to upload a picture of mine... And maybe we might figure out a date..."

Yes, finally a move forward. Two days later, the picture appeared on M's profile page, even though it was out of focus...

"Dear M.
I do see now a blurred picture - is it blurred for everyone or just for me? On some purpose? In this way, I've no chance to recognize you at the market nor any other place..."

Well, in the end there was a picture, based on which I got a very favorable impression, I liked her gentle smile... And thanks to this one picture, we ran into each other as described above (...while I waited in line to get my ticket, I spotted a woman passing by, whom I saw a few days before on a amateurish photograph in her match making profile. Having paid for the ticket, I proceeded to the bar where M. Was waiting to order. I touched her shoulder shyly: "Excuse me, please, aren't you M.?").

How did it work out? We had a date a few days later in a quiet restaurant in the Old Town. We were no strangers to each other anymore, we shared similar philosophy, we had almost the same reminiscences of the eighties in Zürich, and yet there was an invisible dividing wall between us which seemed to hinder any attempt to get closer. No spark there. We set off for home. I accompanied Meret on the nocturnal walk through the town, and once we passed under the railroad tracks, on a dimly lit corner, we cheek kissed and departed. I waited for a while, watching Meret go home but she didn't glance back. I was disappointed.

"Dear Franta,

It was a nice and interesting evening with you, and I'm glad I got to know you. And I would like to keep the contact alive. The conditions of our lives are quite different, especially the everyday routine though - on my part - I find it exciting. Yes, and in regard to the sensuality, that might be rather difficult. No doubt I've noticed how much you're still occupied by your last relation. Some time must pass after all... And I'll join you for a concert occasionally... Now then: Merry Xmas! Love,
Meret"

Writing down this coincidence, almost two years have gone. We meet by a chance, and any and every meeting with Meret makes me happy. We drink a cup of coffee, we drink a glass of wine, and we always have lots to talk about, books, music, life itself... And the "Sensuality"? Yes, rather tricky. Oh, hell...

The Double Pisces Leo Coincidence on August 19, or When the Stars Have a Go

I met my angel on July 1st, 2011, actually an angel with capital A because that is how I am going to call the hospital nurse assigned to take care of me: Angela. I came to the hospital for a controlled heart cardioversion[1] and that required me to be set up for the anesthetic infusion, the attachment of the ECG sensors and the shaving of the relevant areas for the defibrillator. I lied in the hospital bed, my stomach growling from time to time, and I watched the nurse how she moved around the bed in a somnambulistic manner which had me wonder if it was her professional way of doing things or because she just had a sleepless night behind. At any case, Angela did her work on and around my body routinely, and so we were able to strike up an easy conversation soon. I told her the previous steps I went through since 2008 when I was first diagnosed with the arterial fibrillation and subsequently had to undergo - in the meantime - 13 cardioversions and 3 ablations. The nurse listened attentively, and when I finished my "medical history", including the personal situation which caused it, she told me a few bits and pieces of her life. I liked what she told me and how she told me. Angela was happy when she could travel, she was apparently curious to experience other cultures up to the extreme, living together with some

---

1 Cardioversion is a medical procedure by which an abnormally fast heart rate (tachycardia) or cardiac arrhythmia is converted to a normal rhythm, using electricity or drugs.

indigenous people for months. I was impressed. My eyes followed her constantly, I almost forgot why I was there, immobile, covered just by a shirt opened in the back, baby like. What did the nurse, the professional, see? And what did Angela see as a woman? A slightly overweight man, age sixty, hair thinned, the color of hair more white than grey, a few age spots... Apparently having lost any sanity, I realized that I began to be enchanted by Angela. I liked her movements, I liked her green eyes, her black hair, her gently cut face, her radiating femininity in spite of the stiff all white hospital uniform. And on top I was charmed by her soft, tender voice. Foolish me!

At about noon, one by one all other necessary medical personal united around my bed, and finally the chief cardiologist spoke the directive "Let's go." Injected, the anesthetic liquid started to flow into the tube ending in one of my arm veins, and as I was losing consciousness I felt a hand grasping mine. I remember feeling immensely grateful for this unexpected human - I mean angelic - touch, and I responded with equally soft pressure while intertwining my fingers with those of Angela. Then, increasingly numb but holding firmly onto the fingers, I glided away. I have to add that it was for the first time that someone slid a hand into mine during the conversion of the rhythm of my heart. The moment of losing consciousness is a rather schizophrenic affair since on one side you feel pleasant warmth while falling into the absence, yet on the other side you are left with fears about the capital question: "Will I wake up ever again?" So you better, preventively, say "goodbye". By itself it is a serious consideration. It becomes even more so because ahead of every intervention you have to sign a document that states that you are aware of the fact that two percent of these conversions do end lethally. Pondering a prediction for myself, I wondered if I am supposed to multiply the number two by the number thirteen of the already performed conversions, which would make it a chance of twenty six percent. Right, thus purely arithmetically, I might be the "every fourth person" gone.

Well, I came back. I was told by the cardiologist that the conversion went fine, the fibrillation had stopped, my heart was in rhythm, and in a few hours, I would be allowed to go home. Soon we were left alone again, me and Angela. And I have to say that now for sure I was not myself anymore. The feeling of comfort and gratitude while the nurse held my hand stayed with me, and I could not take my eyes off her. Gradually I realized that I fell in love with my nurse. I was unable to think straight, I mumbled incomplete sentences, but finally I was ready to leave. During all our joint time Angela's name tag remained inverse and I felt inhibited to ask for her real name. In the end, I managed to pass on to Angela my visiting card. In the corridor, I turned around to catch one last good-bye glance of her but I slipped off the heel of my summer sandal trying to give a youngish impression. That sure went wrong. And of course, right at that moment Angela came out of the intensive care unit where I was treated, and she saw my comic misstep which ended in a pirouette which was a cross between waving and wobbling. Somehow, I balanced my way out without falling on my nose. Uff.

The subsequent days were filled with a hectic energy of someone obsessed by one idea: how to get to see Angela again? Where to find her? How to approach her? I knew this was hardly an attitude of a man like me, a mature man, his time way over - to be straight, it was purely old men's foolishness that ran me down and over... OK, to cut this angelic story short, I managed to meet Angela and at our second meeting, which was just to be a formal meeting for a few minutes, I was told there was a change of program and we might have a lunch together. Delighted, I nodded and asked her what the occasion was for such a generosity. I was told it was Angela's birthday, and that my company would be something like a birthday present she was giving herself. I know I blushed, and I stayed speechless for a while. Then the only passable reaction I came up with was: "Am I to wrap myself up in some way for you?" Angela didn't laugh, she smiled. Her birthday was August 19.

Angela was living with a friend. I knew clearly I could not dream of becoming his rival. There were 25 years of age difference between me and Angela. Still, in the meantime, there was something which drew us together, I was not alone in this anymore. After the birthday celebration, we met from time to time, we had an intensive exchange not only in person but also by short messages and by letters (only one way, from me to her) which lasted for almost a year. Once we went to the theatre, we exchanged books, I burned music CDs for her (she loved J.J. Cale's "Fancy Dancer"), and a few times we went for boat trips together. What was special was that we could stay quiet and still, not talking, wordless, for hours actually, and at the same time feel each other's soothing presence - simply the greatest feeling I have experienced so far in my life. What was also special about our platonic affinity was the fact that we were able to communicate easily in different languages, using Swiss dialect, German, English, French or Italian accordingly to a raised subject or mood. Angela loved France. To put it boldly, we knew our way about the world, most of the pleasures included. On several occasions I even wrote poems for Angela, kind of a mixture of adoration and desire, a folly, hallucination, like this one...

A Small Pietà

Madonna's, Angela's face
but no lifeless body
on her lap, no Jesus

Her face I hold with
both my hands,
yet not touching it

I kneel down, put
my head on her thighs
the eyes closed

Angela's hand comes
to rest on my head,
quiets all fears

My Angela is mine,
I stay on my knees -
relieved and in peace
My Angela is mine,
and Angela bringing the end
I am free to leave

But suddenly Angela stopped being around. She ignored my short messages and letters. I asked her, desperate, to help me, to tell me to stop! But not even that came in. In one of the last letters I begged her to command, to order me explicitly to leave her alone:

> "...*Provence. No Mistral today! I would certainly love to share this with someone close. I've forbidden myself to communicate with you but as you see, I am too weak a character to hold on to it. Why!? I would really, really love to forget you but you are still around. I see things and immediately I converse with you. Like in Arles where I stood quietly for a while in front of the shop window looking at the blouse... Well, now you have it in front of you. In two months it will be one full year since I've experienced your Angelic touch and since then I'm living under its spell. Maybe you will be the last woman who has broken my heart, and in my situation now I say: 'Why not? There could not be a better, more beautiful one.' The intensity of my feelings towards you cannot be outplayed.*
> *And then, I always end up imagining your previous life, splicing together the bits and pieces you mentioned to me... And I felt like taking a gun and going to punish all the people who have done any harm to you before; in that I am with you, believe me, the more that I've this book project about Brazil. By the way, they all were robbed there, ugly thing, held at gun point but survived... Please, forgive me this letter, and this little cadeau. And maybe you would make it easier for me if you would let me know clearly and once for ever: 'NO MORE, LEAVE ME ALONE!!! STOP IT!!!!!' I would respect that...*"

This was the end, an end without any ado. I was dropped somewhere along Angela's life path. She didn't even glance back at where she had gotten rid of me. There is no concrete date to remember. Well, I had to settle with that, hard times began. Wherever I looked, I didn't see or meet a woman that would be able to rival Angela. I was lost. Weeks, months went by. In the end, I subscribed to an internet matchmaking platform and - yes - by July, one year later, after exchanging personalia through the platform for a few weeks, I met another Leo, my longed-for companion I am now with. And you know what? My new angel is born in the sign of Leo, she is born on August 19, the very same day... Thank you, stars!

I enjoyed knowing Angela and I suffered greatly for it. All those letters, short messages, poems and other signs of love carry stigma of unfulfilled desires, of wishful imagination, simply - of unhappiness. The more bewildered I was when my new Leo - let's call her by the moniker M. - approached me with genuine, pure happiness. I was astonished how simple happiness may be. M. is also able to communicate in different languages and we even added Spanish to our spectrum. We fell for each other from the very beginning, and in spite of our past histories we succeeded to make ourselves free from the past and enjoy ourselves. On the occasion of M.'s birthday, the very first one to celebrate jointly on the famous August 19, she wrote an email to me:

Re: When the birthday wishes are fulfilled...
Hi my dearest,
I had a wonderful birthday. After the first date with a man from S. in B., then a date in S. and the date's follow-up, being picked up by this special car, then coffee and croissant at "Confisserie Züger" in Murten, just before a chamber music concert in the church of Meyriez; fine lunch on the terrace of the hotel restaurant "Des Bains", a comfortable summer drive to S., siesta...
...Un grand MERCI for a wonderful midsummer day,

Yours M., feeling very close to you.

I feel very close to M. as well. And I am grateful to her to take me as I am, a second hand, a used grownup man born in the sign of Pisces. The funny thing is that M. hates Angela, her Leo sister in the Stars, stricken by a retroactive jealousy...

Compatibility of Pisces Man and Leo Woman

Romantic and passionate nature of these individuals waters this relationship to grow to the fullest. The invincible nature of a Leo woman may bind this relationship to cherish the long-term compatibility. If fights are put at a bay then they can enjoy the dish of love every day. A Leo woman and a Pisces man form a supreme love pair. But, sometimes a clash may arouse due to the selfish nature of a Pisces man which may not suit with the generous nature of a Leo woman.

Satan's Mushroom
(Boletus satanas)

In the Fall of 2012, together with my new life companion we traveled to Ornans in the region of Doubs, France, mainly to visit the museum of Gustave Courbet. We stayed overnight at the "La Ferme" in Flagey, a place owned at times by Juliette, Gustave's sister. The famous painter is said to have liked it there very much and that comes handy for the exploitation of the region. "La Ferme" offers four bedrooms, including the bedroom of Courbet himself; the bedrooms carry names like "Chambre Courbet", "Aux Amants", "Au L'autoportrait" or "Au Cerf".

On the second day, sunny and pleasantly warm, and after a luscious breakfast, we decided to hike down to Ornans. The chosen path took us around the famous "Chêne de Flagey", descending along a field and later steep down along the water falls. Going through the forest, we chatted at ease with each other, and inspired by the environment I mentioned that I liked picking mushrooms in the forests back in Bohemia.

"Do you know about mushrooms?" asked my friend. "Pretty well, I think," I answered. And as an example of a treacherous mushrooms I mentioned the Satan's mushroom. At that very moment, I spotted one on the board next to our path. I took out my Swiss army pocket knife, cut off the mushroom near the ground and I showed my friend how quickly it started to change its color to violet.

We continued our walk as far as the town of Ornans,

yet we remained sharp, looking to find some other mushrooms now. We did not spot a single one after that, however, whatever kind, either edible nor poisonous; in spite of
the fact that the path through the thick forest from Flagey
to Ornans is over six miles long. Any explanation?

The Biberman Mural Coincidence

February 21, 2013. The day before I landed in Long Beach, drove through Los Angeles and checked into the hotel Erwin in Venice - 25 years were gone since my last visit to the USA. Picking up the *Free Venice Beachhead* in the bookstore Small World Books, there a title of an article has drawn my attention as if it would have been waiting specially for me: Edward Biberman Mural[1].

This coincidence immediately starts a film of recollections in my head. "Look at this!" I say to my companion, "what a coincidence. I've known Edward Biberman, he is the grandfather of my deceased wife Jennifer. Together with his wife, they used to live up right above Los Angeles, below the Hollywood sign. There Jeniffer had grown up. Let me read it, please".

We left Venice Beach, drove up Highway 1 to Monterey

---

1 *The Story of Venice*, 1941; Venice post office

and finally came up to San Francisco where I met my ex-mother-in-law, and she told me that a documentary film was produced about Edward Biberman (*Brush With Life*, 2005). And who is being interviewed in that film? Two generations of Biberman's relatives, mainly Anne Strick and Jeremy Strick, whose parental background goes back to the filmmakers Joseph Strick and Edward's brother Herbert Biberman, the director of *The Salt Of The Earth*, 1954. "What's the big deal?" you may ask. Joseph Strick happened to be one of the directors of the feature film *The Savage Eye* which sparked the desire in me to make "such" films myself - in Prague, in 1966; as born in 1949, I was a 16-year-old then (see "The Savage Eye")

The Midnight Mass Coincidence 2013

My son insisted to attend the Christmas Midnight Mass at 11 PM, not the one for children at 4:30 PM which I used to take them to before they became teenagers; now they were adults, 18 years old. I told my son, I left the last Christmas Mass I attended because it was incredibly tedious, the sermon full of platitudes, and it went on and on... After an hour, I left the incommodious bench not waiting anymore for the announced concert which I had been looking forward to.

So now, in his first year of adulthood, my son and I went together to the magnificent cathedral in Soleure. The Mass was to be served for the German as well as the Italian speaking community and thus when we arrived, five minutes before eleven, we barely found place in the back rows. The organ began to play and to the general astonishment a group of clowns moved into the church and through the aisle and towards the altar; three clowns on one wheel cycles, two jugglers, a girl swinging hula-hoops and a magician. The clowns reached the proscenium in front of the altar and presented their tricks and stunts with a gusto for quite a while, the ones on cycles moving back and forth through the aisle of the cathedral.

When the clowns left and the organ stopped playing, the parish priest came forward and declared we should not fear there might not be a proper Mass. We should not fear like the shepherds in Bethlehem when the angel told them not to be afraid of things unknown. Then the Mass started and moved on in a traditional way but well dosed with musical entries by the choir and the orchestra. At the very moment when we were told of the birth of Jesus, when Maria has her son in her arms, a baby broke out crying at the back of the church. The holy space resounded with heartbreaking, short pulsed, choking, almost out of breath cry - like if a real new born came to life at this very moment. After a while, when nothing else was heard, the crying receded, the mother carrying her baby outside.

No, this time it was not a staged gag to make the Mass more entertaining, it must have been just a coincidence - though a powerful one. The Mass went on under the spell of its magic, the feeling of Christmas settled among us, and after almost two hours, close to one in the morning, the Mass participants got their blessing and started to spread throughout the peaceful town, enriched in an unexpected, unique way.

A Flea Market Happenstance

A year and a half after I was commanded to leave the family home, I went through a local charity flea market. I like old things, I like to imagine the objects' history. But having reduced my living quarters to a one room apartment, I seldom buy anything these days (and when I do, sooner or later it ends up in the garage). Looking at a long row of framed pictures leaning against a wall, I immediately spotted pictures which used to belong to me, pictures which were created for my film projects, historic costume designs and others. But there was also a small itching, in color, of an old armored Swiss warrior I bought for my son when he was about 10 years old. He kept the picture on a wall in his room, right above his PC. A shattering experience. It felt like I wasn't around anymore, deceased, and the final disposal of my worldly things was being staged.

A few years later, after my son moved out and began living on his own, I passed the Swiss warrior back to him and once visiting his new home, I spotted the small picture leaning on a windowsill above his bed.

My Son a Chancellor

Not knowing it beforehand, I married into the family of a chancellor. The grandfather of my wife was the man who exercised political power during and after WWII. Yes, times long gone.

But his great grandson has difficulty finding himself. My son is 19 years old but does not yet have any apprenticeship nor does he express any interest in higher education. I found an article about such youngsters in a serious life style magazine, and included, there was a test how to find a profession and which one it might be. Filled with curious expectation, I waited for my son's habitual visit for a lunch I cook for him about once a week.

When we finished the lunch, during which I had to chide him - as usual - for eating with his mouth open and gobbling the food too fast, I collected the empty plates and laid the magazine in front of him, inviting him to have a go at the test. To my astonishment my son didn't resist as usual - but started immediately. And he even finished the test before I had time to come back to the table. He pushed the magazine over to me, saying deadpan: "Chancellor."

Here are the test steps and my son's answers one after another:

What do you like to work with?
A) People, plants or animals?
B) Objects?
Neither.

Do you like to talk about current topics?

Yes.

Mainly about sports?

Yes.

Who is the best soccer player in the world?

A) Cristiano Ronaldo

B) Messi

C) What does this have to do with the selection of a profession?

Here my son picked this possible answer:

Nothing at all.

And that was the end of it:

Smart guy! >Chancellor

Location Coincidence

For decades, I have been buying the German weekly *Die Zeit*, published in Hamburg. The newspaper was founded by Gerd Bucerius, and after the end of WWII it profiled itself in a liberal and high culture manner; as follow-up publishers, personalities like the former chancellor of FRD Helmuth Schmidt or Marion Gräfin von Dönhoff stood for these humanistic values. Here is what Wikipedia has to say about *Die Zeit*: "The paper is considered to be highbrow. Its political direction is centrist and liberal, but has oscillated a number of times between slightly left-leaning and slightly right-leaning. *Die Zeit* often publishes dossiers, essays, third-party articles and excerpts of lectures of different authors emphasising their points of view on a single aspect or topic in one or in consecutive issues. It is known for its very large physical paper format and its long and detailed articles."

Every weekly issue has three pages which are dedicated to topics related to Switzerland; in November 2012, my attention was drawn to a full-page article titled *Nachruf auf einen Schweizer (A Life of a Swiss Man)*, written by Dieter Freiburghaus, an independent political analyst. The article presented the biography of a man who lived in a small Swiss-German town and worked as the owner of a hardware store, and whose life span covered about the same period of the 20th century as my father's vita (born 1912 resp. 1909, died 1994 resp. 1986). While reading the article portraying that one Swiss life, which was actually the life of the author's father, I could not help but frequently think about the life of my own father. In the end, I had an idea to borrow the structure of the article and use it to tell the story of my father's life. What struck me most, was the fact that those two Central European men stayed all their lives in one place, Laupen resp. Prague. However, they greatly differed in the number of their nationalities. The senior Mister Freiburghaus got by with just one citizenship in all his life while my father's went through seven changes: he was born as a subject of the Austrian monarchy, became a citizen of Czechoslovakia in 1918; by 1939 he was subject to the Protectorate Bohemia and Moravia, in 1945 he once again became a citizen of Czechoslovakia; by 1948 he was a man of the People's Democratic Republic of Czechoslovakia (ČSR), by 1960 one of the Socialist Republic of Czechoslovakia (ČSSR), and by 1969 of the Federal Socialist Republic of Czechoslovakia (ČSFR)... Yes, that makes seven different citizenships in total. (If my father had lived as long as 1992, he would have become a citizen of the present Czech Republic on top of that.)

When I had finished my version of a man's life, my father's, I approached Mr. Freiburghaus by e-mail and asked him if he would be interested in reading it. I looked forward to his answer. It came swiftly.

"Dear Mister H.,
to motivate someone to do something positive is always a good thing. I'm looking forward to reading your father's biography. Since I'm living in Solothurn myself, we might meet on occasion..."

So, here we have the coincidence: location. The two of

us, the next generation of our diverse ancestors, the author of the article published in Hamburg, Germany, and me, an inquisitive reader, happened to be neighbors living not even a mile apart, in the middle of Switzerland, in the provincial town of Solothurn.

As an afterword, I am quoting here the written response by Mr. Freiburghaus after he had finished reading my article.

"It is amazing how two men of about the same generation and about the same social level have experienced the world in a completely different way. It makes one aware of the fact that Switzerland had a seat in a loge and was just watching. One other difference is of course that I have picked only the special aspects of my father's life which present distinctly the man as bourgeois/ citoyen..."

Upon that I injected that it is quite understandable to sit in a loge being Swiss - and watch. But with me, one question remains open and hurts: "Why was the very heart of Central Europe, Prague, so easily left alone, there behind the Iron Curtain, to become a game of ball to the Russian empire?"

Both articles are available at the link below, though only in German so far: http://galerie9.com/manuscripts/ manuscripts-1/nachruf-auf-einen-prager/index.html

Shifts Happen

On October 17, 1989, a 6.9 magnitude earthquake hit the San Francisco Bay Area, killing 67 people and causing more than $5 billion in damages. On that very day, at 9 PM in the evening, the San Francisco KQED public television aired my documentary *Verne - All Kinds of Lives*. The film, 40 minutes long, shows a portrait of Verne Wells, a San Francisco native who came into the world during the night of the big 1906 earthquake on April 18; Verne was born in a tent in the Golden Gate Park where people were evacuated to from the burning downtown; Verne was born two months prematurely, in the film he remarks that someone still owes him "two months cost and logi in this damned town".

Not many people were watching TV that evening after the second shift happened, which is understandable, hence the publicity the film, and respectively Verne, got was rather low. But a friend of mine organized a party at her home where Verne and his buddies from the Spec's bar could watch the adventurous life story between the two shifts: San Francisco, Los Angeles, Munich, Paris, San Francisco, Stuttgart, San Francisco, N'Djamena, Paris, Rennes and back to San Francisco - in a wheelchair because of a nightly motorcycle accident at the age of 72; no more violin playing, instead an accordion or a synthesizer, no more driving or sailing, instead taking photographs of his friends at his home to be used as such or as templates for oil paintings later on; after he was able to walk again, a nightly stroll from "Casa Costanzo" on Washington Square, along the Bohemian Café, over to Spec's Bar at 12 Adler Lane, or right next door to the café Tosca on Columbus, to chat with Richard Specs Simmons or Carol Doda, smoking at least a pack of filterless Pall Malls a day, and drinking "Holy water", or better, some Pilsner and Asbach Uralt. Verne always enjoyed a conversation, and he was happy to speak with a stranger in his or her language. Verne knew German, French, and Chinese as well as some Spanish and Japanese.

Verne lived until 2001, he reached the age of 95. His ashes are deposited and on display in an empty bottle of "Mountain Rum" in a bar in the town of Sonoma, CA.

Fishing For Coincidences - Hitchhiking

Remembering hitchhiking, it strikes me as a way of fishing for coincidences. You take off, place yourself at the mercy of men and women who assumably have good hearts, who wish for company, who are bored, who would like to show off... So, actually both parties are fishing for a coincidence. Anyway, it was the best way to get to know the United States from the East towards the West, experiencing great encounters, even adventures, lifting up my thumb as well as picking up other hitchhikers when at a certain point, I bought myself a used Chevy Impala for $250, selling it later on for the same price; I was a beat generation kid, a tramp (no insurance).

On one other occasion I was returning from a trip to Victoria Island, hitchhiking on freeway 101, standing on the last ramp leaving Santa Rosa. It was around 4 o'clock in the afternoon when a Japanese made compact stopped to give me a ride. The driver was a man in his fifties, very civil looking, dressed in a business-like suit. I got in, and before we started to move we shook hands, greeting each other quite formally. Hearing our accents, we both realized we must be of the same origins.

"Where are you from?" asked the man.

"Prague, Czechoslovakia."

"Me too," nodded the man and introduced himself: "Havrda"

"Havrda..." I stuttered, in disbelief.

"You mean, you mean your name is Havrda?"

I nodded Repeatedly. Mister namesake was also shaking his head, and smiling. He pushed into first gear and we moved onto the freeway in the direction of San Francisco.

STOP! That is not correct... This countryman of mine, also an emigre of 1968, was no Havrda. His real name was Hora. Sorry, but for years I kept telling this story of meeting my namesake so that in the end I've taken it as true, and now, some forty years later, going through my irregular notes and inconsequent diaries, I've rediscovered that his real name was Hora (si non e vero e ben trovato). So much for this mind of mine, which gave in to this mystification as told so far. But nonetheless, a Czech countryman picking up another one in the USA[1] might be quite a coincidence by itself.

We drove on the 101 freeway towards San Rafael where Mr. Hora was living. He was of extremely fine manners and reminded me of my father, whose age he shared, and whom I had not seen for more than ten years (and was not to see ever again). While driving we kept talking about our refugee lives since August 1968. We became familiar. We both enjoyed each other's company. Mr. Coincidence suggested to take me to his home first, to have a cup of coffee, later he would drive me to San Francisco where I lived. I agreed.

At his tidy home, in a flat of a small apartment house, we set down at a round table and I was offered Turkish style coffee, the way we were used to drinking coffee back in our home country. We picked up our conversation where we had left off in the car, and we exchanged farther details.

---

1 In 1976, the Bicentennial Year, the USA had a population of 218,035,164, Czechoslovskia of 14 million, from which 10 million were Czechs and Moravians. Between 1946 and 1975, 27,048 Czechs immigrated to the United States.

We talked for hours, gradually the night came down on us, until we found ourselves in an almost complete darkness. Of these several hours of conversation, I still remember two things: his wife had died not so long ago, and his daughter Alena studied music in Salzburg. She played piano. Now Mr. Hora was living alone, his loneliness filled his apartment in an almost palpable way; my company did good to him.

Mister Hora drove me home to San Francisco as promised, we shook hands one last time, and he departed back to San Rafael. I don't know why, but I have never met with Mr. Hora again, though I have kept him firmly in my mind - as Havrda, my namesake.

The Velvet Revolution Coincidence

For the first time, I was able to visit Czechoslovakia, Prague, my native ground, on September 21, 1988; on a day exactly twenty years after I had left it following the invasion by the Russian empire, disguised as the Warsaw Pact Armies. I was not looking for this coincidence, it merely took me that long to get my Swiss passport and the entry visa to my old country after having to get rid of my previous citizenship of Czechoslovakia, and after having paid on both sides. On the very first possible day I took off, I was in a hurry to have a look back home, even though my father and my grandmother were already buried without my attendance. Sad times.

Another coincidence in regard to a date occurred a year later, on November 17, 1989. Nine days earlier, on November 9, the Berlin Wall fell.

I was invited to the documentary film festival in Leipzig and on my way there I drove first to Prague, where I arrived - on the evening of November 17 when the demonstration against the regime was suppressed by brutal police force in an artificially created dead end on Národní Avenue. The first night I spent at the wireless at my mother's place, watching the magic eye tube trying to get a clean reception from the jammed transmitters like Radio Free Europe, BBC, and Voice of America. The next day I was in the streets myself.

I was able to stay in Prague for about a week; a week filled with the common anxiety that the party would have the workers' militia disperse the protesters, and later on days and nights filled by growing satisfaction as the party's might began to fall apart and the general public started to get the news about the disintegration directly from the Czech radio and television. In the overcrowded streets of Prague, I met old schoolmates and friends I'd not seen or talked to for more than twenty years (I met two by coincidence, two upon a date). Well, I wasn't active there, in the crowd. I didn't shout or whistle or ring my keys. I was watching the people. I listened to the various balcony speeches. I felt great joy for them (us) but at the same time I asked myself if the twenty years of "normalization" really were necessary in the context of the country's history; it was a completely wasted period of time, of no use for anyone, either in the West nor in the East.

The first free Leipzig Film Festival was special. The life in the streets, in the pubs, and in the churches, was actually more interesting and exciting than the festival program. The GDR government had not totally disintegrated yet, like the one in Czechoslovakia, but the freedom was certainly "in the air". I had returned from Leipzig to Zürich with the resolution not to get involved, not to even think about "going home". I was living in Switzerland, I pursued my work there, I had my friends there, my girlfriend... But when the historical development continued to progress culminating in naming Václav Havel, the playwright and dissident, for president, I could not withstand the lure and I found myself on a train to Prague for his inauguration on December 27.

I stayed for the New Year Celebrations which I won't even try to describe here. But since I happened to be an authentic witness of all these historic changes, I could not resist and I suggested that the Swiss TV make a documentary about the Velvet Revolution as it was called in the meantime, the main aspect of the film to be about the vastly important role students played in the progress and the final success of it.

The Lola Blog Coincidence

Do you have a blog? I don't. But a friend of mine does. He actually has three blogs: *Writing for the Drawer*, *Pillow Talk*, and *Ofgraphomania*. My friend is an extremely good writer, he spots things and he turns them around to find some unique, astonishing aspect of their nature. In short, he is a brilliant observer of things around him. He is funny in his way also. I've enjoyed reading his blogs for more than ten years so far. Here is an example:

Tears on my pillow
Now the pillow's inquiring.

What is this all about? Why another blog by you A.? To contribute even more graphomaniac warble to the industrial noise of the Internet? As an aimless exercise in phonographic writing? Phonography without photography? Who needs that?!
An honest answer in the age of widespread dishonesty. The blog was started as a lure, a bait, a tease, to gain something of some importance then, and in the end of little importance now and in the future. The bait must have been stale anyway, because it didn't succeed in luring the prey, but the blog, begun but devoid of content, stayed.
What to put in it, that is still the question, as its initial purpose was unknown and unknowable. Things that one would only tell or cry to one's pillow? Exhibitionism of the secretive kind? Sounds like a plan, enjoy!

Once I visited my friend's blog but there was no new entry. Frustrated, I was tempted to push the button "Next Blog" and I did so. Immediately I was attracted by the blog's title which was *Time Fuse*, and even more because its owner had a female name: Lola. The coincidence?[1] Lola had been writing in English, yet she was, like me, of Czech origin, the suffix "-ová" placed after her family name gave her away. When I ran into her blog by chance, in the second half of the zero years of the 21st century, she was a student in England, and she was rather enraged by the world around - and herself as well. (Remember the film *Once*? The Czech migrant worker Markéta? And the song which won the Oscar[2]? I pictured Lola like someone similar to Markéta.)

SUNDAY, NOVEMBER 19, 2006

I don't wanna define myself
I don't want to be somebody
I don't want to define myself
I don't want the crowd to judge me
I don't want the judge to judge me
last sentence:
I think Madonna is stupid.

---

1 One infographic (*How Many Blogs are on the Internet*) puts the figure at 152 million blogs for year 2013. Another source (*Number of blogs world from 2006 to 2011 | Statistic*) puts the figure at around 173 million blogs in 2011. Both may have different methodologies for computing the figures, but both sound plausible enough. It's been 20 years since the world's first-ever website (CERN) in 1991/93, and blogs started appearing very shortly after that.

2 2008, Best Achievement in Music Written for Motion Pictures, Original Song For the song *Falling Slowly*, Glen Hansard/Markéta Irglová: https://www.youtube.com/watch?v=bWyhQbxcOIg

I'm cutting the navel cord
my mother doesn't want to do that
she fears blood
so I have to be strong and
get the knife
and gently
slate
the flesh.
How is it possible that they didn't show me the right?
Sometimes I want to arrest them for that. Torture them to death.
I hate all them who act like
having a patent for life
hidden at the bottom of their ward - - robes.
Will I ever?
Will I ever become a woman?
Will I ever penetrate the hymen?
Will I ever kill what's killing me?
I don't want to be a virgin any more.

... I wrote them all in English because it's my second language
and I just like the swing and the cloud on the top of my tongue
it creates. It's still me but it's not at the same time. It's not in a
slightly challenging way. The challenge is sometimes pleasant and
sometimes painful. Sometimes both at the same time. It challenges
the unknown. That's why.

Like my friend A., Lola also had several blogs, the most important was called *So What...*, the other *Blah Blah — BlahBlahblaaaaaah* and *These Days*, later on *Time Fuse*.

MAN
How could I know?
How should I
If you were so closed before
And now you are so different
telling me things
about yourself
and
I can just listen
and
It's so bad
because i want to talk
I want reply
but
my lips are brut
my mouth full of
fatigue
relics
from my previous life
and
feels like shut ()
I sigh to kiss you
all over
your beautiful body
but I tremble to beholden to you.
And if I could
would it change?
because
it feels like it would kill me ...
... Don't I want to die?

oh holy Oneness
is this right?
DO I worship my loneliness more than LOVE?
Blah blah blah…

There's a craft of life here. There's an art of life here. These who can cope with the craft of life are successful and happy. If you master the art of life, it ceases to be important how successful and happy you are.

In these years, my daughter entered the difficult age of adolescence and was even treated for "atypical mental anorexia", and thanks to Lola I could experience my daughter's future years through a magic looking glass. I knew what I had to be ready for (Now, ten years later it seems as if she has overcome this period of becoming a woman without much damage.). Well, I became a fan of Lola. I started to check her blog regularly, and at some point in 2009, I sent her an e-mail:

"Hi there, Lola - if you are the one who has the blog 'Time Fuse', then I would like to get in touch with you. Take care, G."

More than two years went by before Lola finally replied, October '12:

"Hey G.! Yes, I used to write that blog - did you want to say something about it to me? It's been a long time - since both, when I wrote that blog and when you wrote on fb. but I never really used to log in on facebook and the messages were delivered on an e-mail I smashed some time ago (even if I recently realized I still can use it) - but anyway. Do you still want to say

*something I should know? I see you live in Switzerland...? Is it
a good life there, for you? Be well, G., and thanks for getting to
me like this, in reaction to my then-blog :-)*
Lola"

*"Hi there Lola! When I approached you in 2009... How did I run
into you? Your blog was next to the one of my friend in Berkeley,
CA. That chancy, yes. Somehow I've kept returning to your blog
to be part of your rage (kind of your becoming, I guess.)..."*

OK, let's stop right here. I am happy to know Lola, to
know she is fine. Lola became the mother of a girl, and she
is out there making her life, having finished university as
well. My fingers are crossed for her, for Lola, my virtual
chance encounter in the web, for this unique being among
the millions of net users. And what's most pleasant to me
is the fact that Lola can imagine careers or moves of her
life without any ideological, political or economic limita-
tions (No Iron Curtain!!!). In spite of the corruption and
the apparently faulting democracy in the Czech Republic,
Lola is free:

*"...here, among 1000 people you see 995 fed up faces. From time
to time I am really getting mad about it. At least we can travel frequently and so this depression can be ventilated somewhat.
But I also don't want to rot away here... we want to live somewhere else... I want to go to Amsterdam, my man to Asia or
Africa :-D... I don't resist so much ;-), we shall see, what shows
up and when :-)"*

...A long break followed. Until another global coincidence struck me, this time not among bloggers but on face-

book: a few weeks ago, in that right column next to the timeline, there were the ever-changing suggestions to join groups or meet new people you might know and one ad drew my attention: an alias "Šlapenato" an expression similar to the name of a folksy brass band in Bohemia, *Šlapeto* (The Treaders). It somehow reminded me of something I should know… I translated "Šlapenato" as "Go for it". I clicked on it and - see, it's Lola again. So now we have 2016, our lives go on, and our exchange has been picked up afresh… Lola has married, has another name in front of the -ová, and is still going strong.

Would you like to know how many blogs were written today? Visit: http://www.worldometers.info/blogs/

Hospiz zur Heimat
a conclusion

In my coincidence called *Hospiz zur Heimat* ("Hospice At Home" on a street called Justice-Alley) I wrapped it up by saying: "Now I consider this coincidence - the same destiny, the same one room, the same name - the most important one in my life. This very coincidence conjured a lifelong friend for me (thank you synchrondestiny!) and a string that created an emigre DNA, a template as far as my professional career goes."

The hospice was not only a melting pot but also kind of a human seedbed for all my future life steps. There I met my "lifelong friend" of the same name, Jiří, a musician, thanks to whom later on I was introduced to people of a traveling puppet theatre; and thanks to the puppeteers I got passed on to a film company in Zürich where I could start my film making career, beginning as a lighting man. But in this hospice with its meaningful name "home", I also met one other Czech, Hostivít V. who passed on to me the addresses of his old Prague friends who emigrated to California. I also ran into a third important man, Petr S., who became yet another lifelong friend, and some 25 years ago, my second best man. Second in terms of the number of my marriages.

If... If I wouldn't have had the address of a certain Tomáš F. in Berkeley, CA, while I hitchhiked and later on drove a used Chevy across the United States from the East to the West coast and back (by train then), I wouldn't have

met Pavel Beran, thanks to whom I met my big love D..
One evening we went together with Pavel to Spec's Bar
in San Francisco. As we were driving back, past midnight,
across the Oakland Bay Bridge, and farther on Ashby Avenue we spotted a light in the windows of a corner house.
Pavel said: "Hey, let's stop, there is something going on!"
So I parked the Chevy and we knocked on the door. Yes,
there was a feast going on, yes, we may enter… And that is
how I met D., who followed me to Switzerland, and a year
later who I followed to San Francisco, where we got married. Pavel was a special person, a persecuted "long hair"
of Prague; a poet and a friend to Allen Ginsberg during his
stay in Prague in 1965 when the beatnik guru was elected
king of the Majáles, a May 1st student festivity. Pavel is
the guy who is seen in the photograph taken by the STB,
the Czech secret police[1].

Photo: Allen Ginsberg Estate
Pavel Beran, a young poet from the circle around the magazine Divoké víno
(Wild Wine), also met Ginsberg at the Viola. This photo was taken at the
start of May 1965 by members of the secret police while monitoring the two on
Wenceslas Square. Ginsberg acquired the picture from the archive of the Minis-
try of the Interior during a visit to the Prague in the 1990s.

---

1 https://en.wikipedia.org/wiki/StB + http://www.databazeknih.cz/
knihy/vratte-nam-vlasy-47153; photo from http://www.ustrcr.cz/
data/pdf/publikace/bic/ bic0212/034-047.pdf

My friend Jiří moved back to Prague in the meantime ('16), Petr died ('14), Hostivít now lives in Zürich, gradually losing his sight. Pavel is living somewhere in California. The "Hospice At Home" served its fateful purpose in a fortuitous way, I permit myself to say. When I left Prague, I left everything behind: family, relatives, all my school, sports and film friends - most of whom I would see again after some twenty years. There was nobody I could ask for help or advice. At that moment, except for my desperately homesick girlfriend, homesick for Prague, I was by myself, facing a future in a foreign language, in the Western culture, on the free side of the Iron Curtain, known to me, so far, only second-hand from books, films and music. And those accidental friends I mention here, my generation, became the fellows I won and could rely upon - worldwide. And thanks to Erich Maria Remarque and his books like *Three Comrades* or *Arch de Triumph*, we had one common denominator: As genuine emigrants, we also used to drink calvados, the apple brandy from Normandy. Thank you "Hospiz zur Heimat"!

Fishing For Coincidences - A Honeymoon Ride

My urge to get out of the city started back in my home country when - still a teenager of 17 years - I took off to see a vacation sweet heart in the South of Bohemia, in the town of Třeboň. Unfortunately, I was unable to find my way to her place so I hung around the main square for a while, and since I didn't see Marie there by chance, I had to hitchhike back to Prague in a gloomy mood the same day. The other time I set off and made it as far as Slovakia where I spent a night somewhere in a haystack. People were friendly at that time. They offered me some fruit, a slice of bread with lard spread on it, and a glass of water.

My last hitchhiking trip behind the Iron Curtain was to GDR, to Frankfurt upon Oder, to work on a construction site for the steel works there, in Eisenhüttenstadt. I worked there the year before on an organized base, but in the summer of 1968 I went there on my own since I was penniless as a future university student. I took with me my friend Flex who was also in dire need of some cash. Hitchhiking as a pair didn't work well so we split up and made an appointment to meet at the road sign announcing Frankfurt. I got there around noon and waited. When hours passed by, I realized that my friend - who didn't speak a word of German but studied pantomime - might be waiting at another road sign, and I succeeded in getting a ride on a CZ-scooter to the northern city entry, where Flex was sitting in a road ditch, half asleep. Funny? Well, no. No big deal. The real adventure started when we were caught up in Eisenhüttenstadt by the invasion of the Russian troops. We were transported by buses to Berlin and farther on to the railroad freight depot in Dresden where we had to board a special train which brought us back to Prague. No need to hitchhike then.

My first hitchhiking trip in the USA was from Florida to California. That was my real initiation rite, experiencing incredible hospitality all along my route. I was invited to stay overnight, I was welcome to stay for a few days, I was shown the sites people liked in the vicinity of their homes. For example: I arrived in Santa Fe past 8 PM in the beginning of February, it was already dark, and not very warm... There were not very many people in the streets. I caught sight of warm light coming from large windows, and I went nearer only to find out that it was a public library. I entered the building and at the counter I asked the desk clerk about possible places I could stay overnight nearby. A couple was standing at the desk also, deciding which books to check out. They turned around, looked me over, looked at each other, and then the man said: "You can stay at our place, if you like..."

Jack Kerouac wrote the beatnik bible *On The Road* and I've read that book, but when I was hitchhiking it was out of necessity, since I had very little money while studying in the US. The only thing you've got to have in order to hitchhike is time - and to like people.

Living in San Francisco, it was not easy to decide on a good spot for a hitch. Going North, on 101, the best was on Lombard before it started to turn towards the Golden Gate bridge. My first year at the university was quite demanding since during both semesters I signed up for 21 points, meaning a full work load. During the subsequent school vacation time in the summer of 1976 I wished to get out of the town. I wished to make a trip as far as Seattle, where my girlfriend's sister was living. From there I imagined taking a boat to Victoria island and from there to go on as far as Vancouver, Canada.

On the very first day I got past Eureka and, farther on, as far as the border area between California and Oregon where I spent the night on the edge of some small town, in the woods, wrapped in my sleeping bag. The very next morning, while the sun was coming through the haze of the Pacific coast area, I walked over to the nearest roadside diner, washed myself, and had a simple continental breakfast. I then followed the traffic driving North, towards the 101.

To my astonishment there was already quite a line of hitchhikers along the outbound street merging into the Pacific Coast Scenic Byway, as the 101 was called now. I passed all of them, reaching the end of the queue; I might have been about the fifteenth one in that waiting line so I started to stretch my arms and legs, not paying much attention to the passing traffic. Nevertheless, I was different and not only because of my gymnastics. I was the only one who was dressed in black jeans, a white shirt and a black vest. I probably gave the impression of being a waiter. Well, mentally I was prepared for a long wait but to my surprise a car stopped in front of me almost immediately. A mature woman with a naturally sensual appearance leaned out of the car window and, gesturing with her head towards the inside of the car, she said: "Do you want to come with us for a stretch?" I bowed down to her and peered inside to see the driver. Behind the steering wheel sat a man with a Latino face, shoulder length wavy hair, and impish eyes. He smiled at me and nodded in agreement with the invitation by the woman. "Well, sure, OK…" The woman with the attractive, voluptuous body opened the door for me and then slid closer to the driver while patting the empty seat, suggesting that I might sit in the front as well, next to her. I followed her motion and ducked inside, placing my travel bag at my feet. As soon as I closed the door, the car drove off.

"I'm Linda, this is Jacques", said the woman, whose buoyant, feminine manners I got to like immediately. Jacques and Linda might have been around forty. I was about ten years younger.

"My name is Jiri. J, I, R, I,". I spelled my name carefully so that they wouldn't pronounce it as Jerk.

"Oh, where are you from?" asked Jacques, sweeping his long, wavy hair off his face to glance at me sideways.

"Czechoslovakia, originally. Now I'm studying in San Francisco."

"Hey, great J… Jerry", said Linda. "And what are you studying?"

"I have film as my major."

"Wow, nice. And where are you heading to now?"

"I would like to get as far as Seattle…"

"Bad luck, we are not going that far."

"How far are you going?"

Linda looked at Jacques, Jacques looked at Linda, and they both shook their heads. They didn't know - and had to laugh. Jacques pointed towards the glove department and Linda followed. She got out a leather baggie with some grass in it which looked home-grown to me. After she had opened it, she took some cigarette papers out of her shirt pocket and she started to roll a fine, thin joint.

"It's our honeymoon, you know", said Jacques. "We will go as far as our money takes us."

"Just the half of it", added Linda. She smiled and lit the joint, inhaling a little. She passed it on to Jacques. He took it, inhaled lightly, and stretched his arm over to me. The marijuana scent spread around and filled the inside of the car despite the open windows. So I had a drag of the thin joint as well. The joint kept going around in a relaxed, enjoyable manner, like a peace pipe.

"Uhu, well, congratulations to you two", I finally commented on the marriage announcement. "Thank you", said Linda and she leaned over to Jacques. Having pushed his hair aside, she kissed him on the cheek. Jacques nodded, pleased. Then Linda quickly turned to me and pecked me a kiss on the cheek as well. I smiled at her, mumbling almost inaudibly "Thank you, Linda". I looked her over once again, admiring her rich, shoulder long hair which was probably not obedient to her liking.

The car seemed to be floating about a foot above the road, the joint was almost gone. Linda let the roach go out, holding it in her fingertips for a while. What a honeymoon ride, I thought. On the right, woods and barns passed by, on the left Oregon's Pacific beach, brandished by ocean waves. We kept our conversation going at the level of three stoned people, all three of us with a slightly silly smile on our faces. It was a nice stretch of coast, a sandy beach free of human beings kept crawling along like some kind of an endless ribbon.

"Hey, look at that… Can't we stop right here, before it gets too hot?" said Jacques and added: "Soon we should get some gas also." Not waiting for our answer, Jacques crossed the opposite lane to get to the wider dirt board on the ocean side, brought the car to a halt, and switched off the engine. Immediately we heard the waves splashing on the sandy beach, the spume swishing in an irregular rhythm, while the spicy scent of the ocean water filled the car. We stayed quiet for a while.

"Let's go", Linda joyfully prompted, "let's go. I love it." Since I was not really responsive, she leaned across and opened the car door for me. Out there, the Pacific Ocean was spread in front of us in all its vastness. For a landsman like me, it caused powerful emotions every time. Linda slipped off her sandals, furled up her skirt and off she went to wet her feet. Jacques followed her in no hurry and I walked sideward to let them be by themselves. A few feet farther away I found a washed-up wood trunk and sat down in front of it, using it as a backrest. I watched the ocean, I watched Linda coming back from wading to Jacques, embracing him. He embraced her, they kissed for a long time while starting to turn around as if spinning in one spot. "What a honeymoon", I thought, in envy. I always liked woman of Linda's type, the genuine, unpretentious feminine radiation all around her ample body form.

What more is there to say about this coincidence? Jacques and Linda were a happy couple. They didn't have any ambitions (or they had lost them), they worked on a seasonal basis at the fruits farms North of Sacramento, sometimes in canneries. They rented a small cottage in the wood above a place called Berry Creek. They lived on basics, growing their own weed and they certainly radiated contagious immaterial wellbeing. We spent some more time idling on the beach, we exchanged our addresses and it turned out that Jacques and Linda decided to drive back home, insisting that I come to visit them on occasion. Together we walked towards the car, sad because of our coming separation. Here, the honeymoon ride was over for me.

After having done the necessary U-turn, the car of no color and no shine sped away from me, back towards Eureka. Linda as well as Jacques stretched their arms out of their respective windows, waving "good bye". I waved back while crossing the road to hitchhike in the opposite direction up North, up to Seattle, to Victoria Island, to Vancouver, Canada.

A Book To Book Coincidence

"Books have no life; they lack feeling maybe, and perhaps cannot feel pain, as animals and even plants feel pain. But what proof have we that inorganic objects can feel no pain? Who knows if a book may not yearn for other books, its companions of many years, in some way strange to us and therefore never yet perceived?" observed Elias Canetti on occasion. I found this quotation on the web after a book freak told me about it in his own words when I mentioned the occurrence between two particular books on my bookshelf.

Was it a coincidence that Bukowski's *Post Office* stuck next to Brautigan's *Sombrero Fallout: A Japanese Novel*, and this book intimacy, book cover to book cover, enraged my visitor, the author of the Japanese novel who was standing in front of the bookshelf at my home in Zürich?

Richard Brautigan, an author, all of whose books I have read so far, was on the list of the visiting writers at the literature festival in Zürich in November 1983; it was a must for me to go to his particular reading.

Afterwards I ran into him in the spacious corridor of the Mädchen Gymnasium after the rather dull session, and while he was surrounded by other admirers (mostly attractive women), I managed to slip him my visiting card, murmuring: "Just in case you should need something while you are in Zürich." The next day, at about 11AM, I got a call and I was supposed to pick him up at his hotel and we would see what would come up, what we might do. I took Richard around and soon we were on good terms, as if we had been buddies for years. Richard had fun, I had fun. We walked, we ate, we drank, we walked, we drank some more.

That trip lasted about three days and three nights. Richard kind of appropriated me, I was to go with him everywhere: to the dinner at an English professor's place where he had to cook his short story *Cooking Spaghetti Dinner in Japan*[1]. I had to accompany him for the interview for the Swiss TV. He wished to be shown the places James Joyce was supposed to have moved about...

At one point on our first day together we came back to my place to recover. Richard Brautigan made himself comfortable on the spot, falling asleep on the couch, his feet - forever in boots - high on the side board.

Close to the evening the writer woke up and started to look at things. Outdoors the street light had just been switched on and it started to rain. Suddenly, Richard was in a rage. He pulled a paperback out of the bookcase, opened the door to the balcony and threw the book out into the street. I barely managed to glimpse the title: *The Post Office* by Charles Bukowski. I actually liked that book but I was speechless, I had no arguments ready. Richard hissed at me: "You don't need that trash here," and closed the balcony door. I went up to him, curious where the book had landed. It had made it all the way across the street, ending up in the gutter in a puddle along the sidewalk. The book was gradually getting soaked by the rain, and days afterwards I was still looking at it while it was disintegrating

---

1 *The Tokyo-Montana Express*, 1980

slowly, even being flattened by a horse wagon that used to bring beer barrels to the pub on the corner. I wonder if Bukowski would have minded an end like this to a book of his. He probably wouldn't give a damn. He certainly outlived his literary competitor by 10 years. And thinking about the question Elia Canetti raised, if books have feelings, if that should be so, then I certainly feel sorry for the *Post Office*.

Richard went back to the bookshelf. I had pointed out his other books to him. He picked one of them up: *Loading Mercury with a Pitch Fork*. He sat down with it and asked me for a pen.

"I love it, you got this one here...", he said and started to write a dedication for me. The writing was quite distorted by his dyslectic handicap. He wrote: "This is for J. ... Richard Brautigan, Zürich, the unforgettable, November 30, 1983".

Richard and I were friends for only a few months - not even a year later, in September of the following year I was shocked to read in the magazine *TIME* that Richard Brautigan was found dead in his house in Bolinas. It said: "DIED. Richard Brautigan, 49, gentle, low-key novelist and poet of the California underground, whose offbeat books, including A Confederate General from Big Sur (1965), The Pill versus the Springhill Mine Disaster (1968) and the bestselling Trout Fishing in America (1967), offered countercultural youth of the hippies era kind of "natural high" with intense evocations of humor, romance and love of nature; of apparently self-inflicted gunshot wound; in Bolinas, Calif. A badly decomposed body, identified at week's end as Brautigan's, was found in his home by two friends who had become worried about not hearing from him for several weeks." (November 5, 1984)

A Factual Coincidence

First I found Joseph Conrad's *Heart of Darkness* in my local public bookcase, then a few days later, after having
reread the book, I came across the diary of the shooting
of *Apocalypse Now* written by Eleanor, Francis Coppola's
wife. And finally I watched the film again, the redux version of 2001... Strongly impressed, I typed "Kurtz" into
the search line of my browser. Immediately I got the link
for the parting words of Kurtz with his final message: "Because it's judgment that defeats us...":

Watch it here:
https://www.youtube.com/watch?v=KxLFdJLSho8

Threefold Bad Luck (The Second Secondhand Story)

My boyhood friend B. (shot-put and poetry) decided to marry his Dutch sweetheart in Prague shortly after the Velvet Revolution brought Václav Havel up to the castle above his native town, in the function of the president of the now free republic of Czechoslovakia. B., who was not able to visit his home town for more than twenty years, imagined the month of May as the proper season for a wedding, and he also wished and demanded to be married in the Gothic hall of the City hall of the Old Town district of Prague (Prague 1 district). OK, this really happened, he succeeded in getting a ceremony term on short notice thanks to his manly charm and he also succeeded in getting the necessary affidavits from the central registration office (not without using certain physical force). I swear, all this is true for I was his best man.

Before I move on with the actual story of mine, I might pass on to the reader just one bureaucratic detail regarding the marriage legal matters - how do you think the Czechs were going to deal with a Dutch name like "van de Kracht"? Was it to be "van de Kracht-ová?"...

It was an extremely beautiful day, May 1st. It worked out fine: B. and M. got married in the City hall, they had their welcome drinks close to the river Moldau, and they had their wedding party at Nebozízek, the restaurant located on the slope of Petřín Hill from with a gorgeous panorama view of old Prague, from the Castle, over the Charles Bridge, to Týnský Cathedral and the National Theater.

But then the "Bad Luck" started to obscure their Bohemian happiness. They started to come back down to the city of Prague where they stayed at the home of B.'s mother, in the city section called Žižkov, in honor of the war lord of the Hussites in the 15th century. They arrived from Amsterdam in a small compact car and parked it in front of the house, but the next morning the car was gone. This was a case for the insurance company but there had to be a protocol set up, issued by the police. The stolen car didn't show up, so for the next visit a few months later on, B. and M. drove in using another car which they bought to replace the stolen one. Well, the next morning, this car was gone as well... B. went to the police station. The policemen just raised their heads, looking at him in disbelief, until one of the officers asked him if he didn't steal the cars himself... My "shot put" friend (no poetry on that occasion) had to be held back by all present men at the station; he really didn't like this kind of joke being made on his account.

The third stroke of bad luck hit B. and M. when they decided to fly to Prague and to rent a car there. They did so, and driving towards the South where B.'s mother owned a small country cottage, they were hit from the back by a speeding BMW, which had them end up in a provincial hospital about 50 miles south of Prague.

As I've heard from B., his wife, the Dutch tough lady, for her part, is not willing to visit the Bohemian realm anymore ever - easy to understand, I guess.

The Three LoL Coincidences

After the Russian invasion in August of 1968, all together there were about 100,000 emigrants that left the country within a year. They had family names like Voříšek, Houžvička, Růžička, but there were also those whose names provided no pronounciation difficulty: Wagenknecht, Lehmann, Hase. One of the easy to emigrate names was a certain Anna Neumann. I got to know her while working for a Swiss Communication Company where she had an office one level above me because she was an engineer and I was only a technician. We used to meet at lunch time in the canteen, a bunch of Czech emigrants, and whenever Anna joined us, we had something to laugh about. It was her nature to laugh, she just started to talk and soon it turned into some giggling, some side comment uttered, which was picked up by the others and on and on it went...

Soon Anna, being really smart in her field, made herself independent and started to free-lance, later on founding her own company. If you would have met her, you would face a rather tall and broad person, round face with a big mouth and clever eyes, framed by a hair cut in the style of the roaring twenties - a face always ready to burst into a laugh. We became friends in our free time. Once we even spent New Year's vacation skiing in the Alps. A group of young people ready for any kind of nonsense, certainly ready to laugh together with Anna.

As time went by, we all dispersed into other towns,

countries, even continents, more or less losing contact with each other. So the more enigmatic it was to run into Anna years later.

The first chancy encounter happened in San Francisco. I was invited to a private place on Washington Street near Van Ness, and as soon as I entered the living room I spotted Anna. She leaned back, covered her mouth in surprise, only to burst in a loud laughter which I rendered. We exchanged some words in Czech and our laughs kept filling the room... The situation became rather embarrassing because the present Americans didn't understand what was going on, probably taking us for some lunatics.

The second chancy encounter happened about twenty years later, in Prague, when I entered a small Photo shop on Spálená street and there was Anna, her back towards me. She was controlling the prints which were taken - at her wedding. I approached her and bowed over her shoulder to have a better look, in a kind of provocative move. Anna jolted back, immediately covering her mouth in surprise, only to switch over into a burst of laughter.

The next time I was exposed to Anna's contagious laughter by a chance, happened near Zürich, at a restaurant on top of the Albis mountain pass. In the plain sun shine and sitting next to her husband, Anna smiled seeing me coming, only to burst into her boundless laughter - for the last time I was to enjoy.

THE UNBEARABLE LIGHTNESS
OF FORTUITY
38th Pocket, The American One

The Unbearable Lightness Of Fortuity

"For some people, the film *The Unbearable Lightness of Being* as well as Kundera's novel might remain the only true picture, and maybe even the only testimony, that keeps up the memory of the Prague invasion."
                    - Jean-Claude Cariére, *Les années d'utopie*,
                                        Plon, Paris, 2003

To tell you of this particular fortuity, I have to start with the obituary of its main character, the judge of the San Francisco Superior Court, John B. O'Donnell. As published in the *Stanford Lawyer*[1], and in *SFGATE Obituaries*:[2] "John B. O'Donnell '41 (BA '38) of San Francisco, Calif., died on October 6, 2005... After graduating from law school, John practiced with the firm of Littler & Coakley. In October 1942, John enlisted in the U.S. Army, and he served in Europe with the Counter-Intelligence Corps attached to the 330th Regiment, 83rd Infantry Division[3] (Enlistment Term: For The Duration Of The War Or Other Emergency, Plus Six Months, Subject To The Discretion Of The President Or Otherwise According To The Law.) He

---

1   http://law.stanford.edu/wp-content/uploads/2015/07/sl74_articles. pdf, page 44

2 Published in San Francisco Chronicle from Oct. 9 to Oct. 12, 2005 - See more at: http://www.legacy.com/obituaries/sfgate/obituary.as-px?n=John-Baldwin-ODonnell&pid=15315804#sthash.W1Oeutxw. dpuf

3 https://www.youtube.com/watch?v=CRFytde1sGM&feature=share

was in the invasion of Normandy, and served in Brittany, Luxembourg, Belgium (Battle of the Bulge), and across Germany toward Berlin. He received a field commission in 1944 and was part of U.S. Occupation Forces in Bavaria until November 1945. Moving back to San Francisco in 1946, he returned to private law practice. In 1973, he was appointed as a San Francisco Superior Court commissioner, serving as a probate commissioner, hearing officer at the Youth Guidance Center, psychiatric hearing officer for the court, and temporary judge during his years with the court. He was also a 50-year member of the Olympic Club, a devoted 40-year member of the Family Club, and an active member of its Literacy Group..."

One

Thirty years before John B. O'Donnell died, at the end of July 1985, I found myself in San Francisco in order to carry through my divorce from my beloved Californian wife. I was able to stay in San Francisco for only four days, arriving from Yellow Thunder Camp in the Black Hills of South Dakota, and having to be in New York on the following Monday evening. My wife waited for me at the airport and brought me home where I was taken care of with so much love and tenderness that I immediately felt like having arrived at home, *the* home. I was totally exhausted after having slept in a tee-pee for a fortnight, overwhelmed by the impressions of the Lakota Indians' past and present, and going through everyday arguments with the crew in my position as a supervising co-director with Gines Serran Pagan, and/or just waiting around for what Russel Means might decide to do or not to do that day.

Now, after having refreshed myself with a shower and slipping into a loose kimono, I was sitting at a simple table in a Victorian house on Filbert Street in San Francisco, my wife serving me my favorite clam chowder that she cooked herself. We were sitting face to face, both eating the soup, and we didn't do much talking in spite of the fact that we had not seen each other for about five years. From time to time our eyes met silently above the soup bowls, cherishing each other's rare company. We both knew that tomorrow our union would be officially terminated on the base of my wife's request, in order to set me free so that I could apply for Swiss citizenship (it sounds complicated and it was. It is, nowadays, even more so if you are stateless). We drank some red wine, I told my wife a few stories from the Black Hills, and soon we went to bed to cuddle, and to fall asleep, tightly embracing each other. We slept deeply, deeply as if forever.[1]

The next morning, we had a silent breakfast, somehow in the understanding of things waiting for us that day, the day we were getting divorced. We stood around the kitchen, drank our coffee, silently smoked early cigarettes, from time to time glancing at each other. Looking back, it was eight years since when left to get married in Reno in a rush, so that I could apply for US naturalization.

Finally, we set off to seal our separation, which had lasted for eight years, on paper. Our relationship lasted for eleven years in reality, yet lasts up till now because my wife was to die of cancer in 2003 at the age of 49.

We entered the San Francisco City Hall and started the search for the court where divorces were handled. Soon we got lost in the maze, asking for directions left and right. My wife was rather passive, her movements almost somnambulant, and her verbal facilities restrained, as if she were handicapped. Finally, we were shown into the waiting room of a judge's office; we took a seat on the two last free chairs in the middle of the fifth row. Every row was occupied by about seven men and women. We sat there in complete solitude, sitting without stirring: an exercise in patience and perseverance. Unfortunately, we could not figure out the system by which people were respectively entering the

---

1 Kundera says: "Love does not make itself felt in the desire for copulation (a desire that extends to infinite number of women) but in the desire for shared sleep (a desire limited to one woman)." page 15

actual office. My wife was resting her head on my shoulder, we held hands.

"Honey, I have to leave," she whispered to me, "I got to be at work at two..."

I looked at her, into her eyes, and I just nodded. My wife gave me a gentle kiss on the cheek and stepped out of the waiting room. The afternoon hours dragged by, Friday afternoon hours when everyone was already somewhere else in his or her thoughts. But not me, I was nervous as hell. I knew, I just had this one chance, I had to have the divorce legalized by Monday, before my flight to New York, and then farther on to Europe, to Zürich, where I had my stateless residency. The last person had gone into the office and I was left alone in the waiting room. A bell sounded five o'clock somewhere nearby. The last person came out after a rather short period of time, ignoring my presence. "And now?" I asked myself in despair.

There was no one left around anymore, the judge himself was coming out of his office, locking the door. I sprang up, bringing myself to his attention. He was still occupied with the door. As he was locking it he looked at me over his shoulder and asked "What is it?...", as if he wanted to say: "What the hell are you still doing here, my time is over?"...

"I need a divorce, please..."

Having locked the door, he came closer to me and looking at his wristwatch he said: "But not today, not anymore." Before I had time to start my plea for him to make an exception in my case, I stretched the papers towards him, and he reached for them. It must have been the blue Nansen Passport on top of the papers that caught his attention. It was the booklet type of passport, larger than the normal ones, marked diagonally by two black stripes, instead of displaying a symbol of a specific country, titled TITRE DE VOYAGE (Convention du 28 juillet 1951). He lifted the papers closer to his eyes, taking the Nansen passport out of the plastic folder, holding it separately from the divorce form which he examined. He halted: "But your wife is filing for the divorce, not you!"

"Yes, but she had to go to work. And I am leaving for Europe, I have a flight booked for New York, on Monday..."

He gave me back the folder but kept the passport, leafing through its pages as if he had worked at a border Patrol all his life.

"Jiri..., Prague...", he said, and he pronounced my first name properly. "You must be Czech, aren't you?"

I nodded. He smiled to himself, turned around, and stepped back towards the door to his office.

"Come along, OK, come with me," he said and unlocked the office door again.

The judge was a man of middle height, of fine facial features, with a slightly protruding chin. He had attentive, deep set eyes and regarding his age, he might have been my father.

We sat down at a conference table, a window was behind him. He asked, I told him. He nodded, still not looking at the divorce papers. He started to tell me...

"Yes, I know Prague. I was stationed in Bavaria, enlisted with the US Occupation Forces. I used to go to Prague, occasionally. I liked to go there."

"So far, I cannot go there," I interjected. "Since my departure in 1968, for almost 17 years now..."

"That bad."

"I'm now able to apply for Swiss citizenship, and I did

so, but I was told that as long as I'm married, my wife would have to apply also... That does not make sense since we are not living together anymore. That's why I need the divorce."

The judge nodded in understanding though frowning a little bit. I started to wonder where his empathy came from - and how it would go...

"I've just finished reading *The Unbearable Lightness of Being* by Kundera - did you happen to read it?"

"Oh, yes. For sure. It's the story." I said. "In a way, my story also."

"It's a great book, in my opinion."

"Well, in mine as well. I think that Kundera really is covering what it's all about. This violation, the humiliation of a nation... Kundera himself left Czechoslovakia in '75, he has tenure in France, at a university in Rennes..."

The judge was nodding again, signaling he knew, I didn't have to tell him. It was Kundera's book that gave us the subject to talk about, in which the judge was more than interested and - knowledgeable. The year right before, in 1984, the novel was published in English as well as in German.[2] Here I have to add that our exchange at that time, July 85, was based solely upon the books, not upon the film[3] version which Phil Kaufman did three years later, in 1988, starring Daniel Day-Lewis and Juliette Binoche; script written by Jean-Claude Cariére. I quoted the script

2 In Czech published first by '68 Publishers, Toronto, in 1985 and 1988, in the Czech Republic first in 2006.

3 In a note to the Czech edition of the book, Kundera remarks that the movie had very little to do with the spirit either of the novel or the characters in it. In the same note he goes on to say that after this experience he no longer allows any adaptations of his work. https://en.wikipedia.org/wiki/The_Unbearable_Lightness_of_Being

writer at the beginning of this chapter because I am equally convinced that the book "may remain the only true picture, and maybe even the only testimony, that keeps up the memory of the Prague invasion"; next to Cariére's other observation which he states right in the beginning of his 1968 memoir: "The young ones of 1968 won't ever get old. They stay young by definition. Forever."

"...At the end of WWII I was stationed in Bavaria, and from there we frequently made trips to Prague. What a magnificent town! And contrary to Germany, it was not badly damaged. Life in Prague became civil rather quickly. And people liked us, the Americans. What a pity I didn't make it back there, so far. Well, after the Russian invasion in '68..."

"I have not been home since then, I told you already, I haven't seen my father since. My mother was allowed to visit me twice so far. Once after 5 years, and then another 8 years had to go by. Now, when she's retired she might get permission more frequently, but she cannot leave my father alone..."

The judge didn't ask for details, why or why not. He gave me the impression of a well-informed person. And suddenly I recalled another situation when I was dealing with a US authority: actually, during the marriage procedure in Reno, in July '77. There, the female clerk behind the counter, with a blank face resisting any description, with no facial characteristics to mention, went over the marriage form. Suddenly she barked at me: "Cze-cho-slo-vakia! Where the hell is it?!"

Here, with judge O'Donnell it was different, much different.

"You know, I feel a great sympathy for your people there,

for your culture... Music, literature, architecture... Dvořák alone. Or Kafka, and Kundera... Mucha, Kupka..."

The judge leafed through my refugee passport once again. Practically every page had a visa stamp from some country. As a refugee with residency in Switzerland, one had to have a visa to every country, except for the neighboring Austria, Germany or Italy.

"I see, you do quite a lot of traveling... What is your profession, actually? Here it says 'technician'."

"Yes, but not anymore. I always wished to make films... I earned a BA degree in films from San Francisco State. Then I returned to Switzerland; there I started doing documentaries, my own projects. And commercial ones to survive. I'm freelancing - but no feature films so far..."

"I guess, to make a film on the bases of the *Unbearable Lightness of Being* might be just the stuff for you," the judge said smiling.

I shook my head, denying that kind of aspiration: "I certainly can't reach up to Milos Forman or the other Czech directors like Passer, Jasný or Němec. But, for sure, the subject is on my mind. I have had a lot of reoccurring dreams where I return to Prague and then, when trying to leave the country, I cannot, because I've lost my passport or been busted by the police... Those kinds of nightmares. Well, now almost twenty years have gone by and those dreams aren't so frequent anymore."

"So, would I know some of your documentaries?"

Again, I had to shake my head in denial. I told him I did a documentary for UNICEF on social issues, traveling a lot, and some on art..."

"And what's your next project?"

I took a deep breath, collecting my thoughts, mainly

not to sound as if I was boasting about it. I started to tell him about the project in the Black Hills: "I flew in to San Francisco yesterday, to get the divorce here, as I have a few days between shooting in the Yellow Thunder Camp, South Dakota, and editing in New York. As I said, I have to leave San Francisco on Monday afternoon, it's all booked, people are waiting for me there, in New York."

"Yellow Thunder Camp... Yes, I've been reading about it, Sundance Festival, danger of forest fire... Russel Means, right?"

I nodded in agreement.

"How does a man of your origin get to do a documentary about American natives?"

"It's a coproduction. The leading personality is Russel Means, yes, the leader of the American Indian Movement. His Spanish blood brother Gines Serran Pagan - he is an ethnologist with the UN, a painter and a sculptor - he was able to get the consent to stay in the camp, to do some interviews, and in the end to cover this year's Sundance Festival as well; but not the ritual itself, the ripping of the skin, not that... And the Swiss co-producer hired me to co-direct; or rather, supervise the filming; Gines has no background in that field."

"So, you're fine in Switzerland... Why didn't you stay in the US, after your film studies?"

"For different reasons... After the first semester, I realized I'm missing Europe. The four seasons, the different languages, and since I got to know the situation here in the movie business, I didn't see any chance for myself. So, knowing that after two years being out of the country, I would lose my Swiss residency, though not the asylum, I decided to do the BA degree in film in those two years."

"And you did so?"

I smiled a little, dispersing his doubts: "Yes, I managed. I got some special permissions to be able to get more points per semester than normally allowed."

"How did you finance that? With that kind of academic load, you wouldn't have been able to work next to the program, I assume."

"No, I didn't. I was fortunate to have a scholarship from Switzerland. Although, the major part of it I had to pass on as a non-resident tuition... My friend, my wife, also helped me to get through. We shared the rent..."

Almost imperceptibly the light in the room changed while we talked. The fog must have moved into town. The softened light had the power to create an atmosphere of confidence, and a certain intimacy began to reign between the judge and me. First I was nervous, afraid he might kick me out, my affair unresolved, but once we sat down at the table, the tension disappeared. The judge didn't appear to be in a hurry, he listened and he asked questions way over the spectrum of the concern for my divorce. In spite of the fact that his work quota had been filled for the day, for the week, he was still interested in my story.

"You got married in Reno, people from San Francisco usually don't go to Reno to get married...", the judge remarked, once again scanning the divorce sheet with the look of a professional.

"That's the crazy part..." I threw in. Now, on the spot I had to decide if I was going to tell the truth, to explain the scheme behind my marriage in Reno. I looked the judge into his attentive eyes, and recalling his affection for the Kundera book, I brought my marriage story forth, bluntly.

"We did it just for the papers, for the chance I might

see my parents, back in Prague. It was a marriage out of the blue, so to say, just three days before our definite separation, before my return flight to Switzerland, which was already booked. You're a judge, you'll understand. Kundera does not mention a word on this subject, his characters cross the borders back and forth, he omits the question of a passport or a visa totally. But actually, this is the greatest drama a refugee goes through. Papers. That's what he's dreaming about, a nightmare"

"I really would appreciate it if you would care to explain."

"I'll be glad to do so."

The judge stood up, he walked towards the large window and he looked out, his back turned to me. "Just go on, I'm listening", he said to assure me I had his attention.

Two

"Sorry, but I have to begin back in 1974", I went on. "That's when I was able to visit the US for the first time, and that's when I met my wife, Jennifer. When I fell in love with her... And believe it or not, after I returned to Europe, I courted her, so to say, with many love letters. Six months later she got on a plane and flew over to me in Switzerland. Well, actually, she took the cheapest flight possible which was to Luxembourg by Islandic Airlines; I drove up there to pick her up..."

A film ran in my head of that year with Jennifer in Europe: constant improvisations, living in the country as well as in Zürich; me working irregularly, free-lance, she doing theatre and pantomime together with friends of mine. We had a VW bus we were able to travel around in so I was able to show her Florence, Rome, Naples; we even got as far as Taranto. With the theater people she visited Spain and she even had the courage to visit my parents in Prague, twice. I won't ever forget when she stepped out of the train from Prague the second time, with my mother's dark red cashmere scarf wrapped tightly over her hair. But these fragments of memory I kept for myself, at least for the moment.

"To make it short, within a year I was able to get all the paper work done for the admission to San Francisco State and Jennifer took off ahead of me to find us a place to live. We were both on very low funds and had to live on the basics. I had my scholarship but she had to find a job first.

So in the end Jennifer rented a one-room apartment on Valencia, South of Market, and I joined her there by the end of August 1975. You see, I'd always dreamed of coming to California. I grew up under the communist ideology, to learn Russian was mandatory beginning the age of ten, yet I read American writers like London, Steinbeck and Saroyan, later Ginsberg, Kerouac, Brautigan and Ferlinghetti. With literary works bound to California, I grew up in Prague in the sixties. Imagine, in 1965, Allen Ginsberg landed in Prague by chance, being expelled from Cuba on the spot, put on the first plane leaving Havana. I was sixteen years old…"

I realized I was getting carried away, and I interrupted my excited speech. Maybe the judge didn't care for these kinds of representations of California life, I thought. But the judge just said: "Amazing." He shook his head and smiled at me. I smiled also, relieved. Then I picked up the line. I returned to my coming to America.

"Soon after I had arrived in San Francisco, and practically as soon as I had my own address on Valencia, I got an anonymous post card from Washington D.C., handwritten in a very tidy upright style; in Czech it said something like this:

'Dear sir, I do not know you but I have to send word from your mother: do not return to Czechoslovakia because you wouldn't be allowed to enter the field of your activity at all. You would not have any chance because everything is organized and strictly controlled.'

There was no signature. Some good soul on an official trip to the United States spared eleven cents to let me know

I should not even think about going back home. But was it still home, this country? Surely not, and I had no illusions about it. But still I wished to visit at least to see for myself and to see my aging father, to say good-bye - probably for good. And these desires of mine were the reasons for my marriage in Reno, out of the blue, two years later. My very best friend, a US citizen as such, was to marry me, me the stateless one, three days before my definite return to Europe so that - theoretically - I would become a US citizen myself within - again theoretically - two years. In this way, I would be eligible for US citizenship two to three years before I might be eligible to apply for the Swiss naturalization; Switzerland was the country where I enjoyed the refugee status and where I had my residency - and have so far. It all sounds rather complicated, now even to me, and it really was, no doubt about it..."

The judge was still standing at the window, looking out over his hometown. He was listening, I was sure. So I carried on, remembering the succession of events that particular day, more and more details coming back to my mind.

"It started very unexpectedly, by a phone call, a phone call from a student friend of mine, a German: 'Hey, did you read it in the newspaper today?'

'What?'

'About Czechoslovakia. An amnesty was proclaimed there!' The voice of my friend sounded excited to tell me the unexpected news.

'An amnesty - on what condition?' was my immediate reaction.

'That it does not say...,' my friend seemed to calm down.

'I am sure there are some tricks, believe me.'

'Well, do you want to read it yourself? I could bring it to

you. I have to drive downtown anyway.'

'Don't bother. I will fetch the newspaper myself. Thanks.' I told Brigitte, the film student from Germany who was never to do any films, like most of us. After we hung up I felt the inner tension rising. Jennifer was not at home, I could not discuss it with her, I had to run downstairs to the liquor store on the corner of Market and Gough. Just across the street there was one of those newspaper boxes. By now I was excited myself, curious to read the lines though I knew very well that there wouldn't be much more than Brigitte had told me on the phone. The lack of detailed news from Europe, the lack of based information was a constant source of frustration while living in the US.

I put the quarter into the slot and pulled the newspaper out of the box. I found those few lines, reading them for myself for the first time: 'Czechoslovakia's president Husák proclaims amnesty. The communist president of Czechoslovakia, occupied by the troops of Warsaw Pact Armies, proclaimed general amnesty...' Etcetera, etcetera..."

The judge was still standing at the window, his back turned from me. I had the urge to explain. If anyone would follow these procedures, it would be him, so I was thinking and so I kept talking:

"In the summer of 1977, the communist president of Czechoslovakia, Gustav Husák, declared a general amnesty for those who left the country illegally and were subsequently sentenced in their absence for between six months to two years in prison. It is now almost impossible to imagine a law making criminals out of citizens of their own country just by a paragraph in its codex of justice. So these illegals, these criminals like me were to be grandly pardoned by the president. But there was a catch to it:

first, one would have to legalize his or her relation with the Czechoslovak Socialist Republic, his country of origin. And the condition to be able to do so was that one had already acquired a new citizenship of some other country. As a lawyer you might be interested to know the exact premises - and advantages - of US citizenship when compared with other countries; except for Switzerland, where twelve years were required for naturalization. Most other countries asked just for five years of residency before being eligible to apply. Now, having become a foreigner even in relation to the original country, you wouldn't get an entry visa unless you had 'legalized' your status, which meant to buy yourself free from Czechoslovak citizenship; you were charged according to your acquired educational level. But this business they could not apply with a new US citizen because there was a dual citizenship treaty between the countries. Signed in 1929, the agreement prevented dual citizenship of Czechoslovakian citizens who became naturalized in the United States, and *vice versa*, of United States citizens, who became naturalized in Czechoslovakia."

"Is that so...", said the judge and walked across the room, shaking his head in disbelief, returning with a glass of water from the office water dispenser. He gestured to me to drink and to go on.

"Well, my young and unreasonable urge was to fulfill that condition as a US citizen; then, being married to a US citizen, I might apply for naturalization in two years and, on top of that, as a penniless student, I would not have to repay the cost of my education. But who would care for details?"

The more I kept talking, the more I was losing any kind of restrains, and I even felt an impulse to get into "my" story: "So, with *The Chronicle* folded under my arm, I entered the liquor store to get some beer - and to share my excitement about a possible visit to Prague. As a regular customer, I knew Fred, the liquor store owner, pretty well after having lived in the neighborhood for two years, so I spilled the thrilling news out to him: 'Fred, I might go home...'.

'Really? Where did you say you come from - Russia? No, Poland, right?!'

'Czechoslovakia', I shook my head.

'Hmm. Cze-cho-slo-ve-nia... I see.'

'OK, Fred,' I said, 'something like that.' And in despair, I almost sneered at him: 'I will send you a postcard then - if I get there.'

'When are you going?'

'Oh, in about two years - I have to get married first.'

'Are you kidding me?'

I laughed and went to pick up a six pack of the only enjoyable beer I had discovered so far: *Mickey's Big Mouth*. I had to have one." I stopped telling my story rather abruptly now, looking at the judge, but he just smiled and, again, he encouraged me to keep going: "Oh, yes, I know *Mickey's Big Mouth*. I think one *Mickey's* might do us good right now, but... We're not in a movie here, I don't have booze in my office. Just go on, you're quite a good story teller, go on."

"Sometimes repeated scenes of everyday life get kind of burned onto your retina: This homey liqueur store, Fred in his red apron, grabbing a brown bag large enough to put a six pack into... Back home, waiting for Jennifer, I was restless, pacing up and down the double room from one end to the other. When the beds were put upright, there appeared mirrors above the benches. And when the sliding door was open between the two rooms, the mirrors opposite to each other, mirrored themselves. I was pacing in the middle of it all, caged by mirrors... I was completely obsessed by the idea of going home for a visit - in only two years' time! At the same time, I wondered why we could not stay together, I still felt the strong bond between Jennifer and me. To be on one's own, as a "homeless person", a woman was more than a girlfriend; she had to stand for mother, friend, lover, classmate, angel... She was to offer home as well as a peer group identity; some kind of a promise, some kind of a dream to live up to..."

I was getting carried away, I realized, and I stopped abruptly, probably blushing. Silence.

"And then?" asked the judge.

"Well, some time later the phone rang. It was Brigitte again. 'What are you going to do? Jennifer should marry you. I will take you up to Reno...' My classmate seemed to be equally obsessed.

'Brigitte, you know we are splitting. Why should she do this? It is hard enough for her.'

'She is an old friend. She will do it for you, I am sure.'

'Look, even if she would do it - I got the plane ticket already. On the fifth I am going back', I said resolutely. 'I don't have time to get married. And no money either'

'Talk to her. We can go tomorrow', insisted Brigitte.

Well, that's it. That's why we got married, practically on the day of our separation. But we stayed close, very close. Jennifer is a very generous person, big heart. Then our paths divided, me being fully involved in starting my film making career, in Switzerland, etc. I never applied for the US naturalization, and in the end, more than twelve years have gone by now and I'm eligible for the Swiss naturalization. But they won't complete the process unless I get the divorce; I told you, they are afraid Jennifer might apply also. Switzerland does not allow for dual citizenship."

"I see. Some kind of a sleeping 'Catch 22' you got there. I think even Kundera might find your story inspiring or intriguing; I certainly do."

"Believe me, I would prefer an easier way to go through life; and I still cannot go back, even for a visit. Maybe next year, assuming I'll get the divorce, provided I've the court decision with me…"

"Don't worry, we'll do it."

I raised my eyes up to him, apparently with an expression of someone against whom the charges were dropped. The judge smiled at me. But he quickly asked yet another question: "And then what? What's the follow up? What are the farther legal steps waiting for you before you can visit back home again?"

"First I'll have to pay for the Swiss naturalization; on the federal, on the canton, and on the city of Zürich level. Then, having the Swiss passport, I'll apply for the annulment of my Czechoslovakian citizenship - and to pay for it as well. When the Ministry of Interior approves my request, I may apply for an entry visa as a Swiss national."

"Quite a legal battle across many borders. And expenses, for sure…"

"You know, there is yet another aspect to it. I had friends who broke down, homesick. I'm not worried about myself but these fates get to you. For example, one of my refugee friends decided to go back, he was in a panic and disregarded the paragraphs made for someone who stayed abroad without permission - it was called 'illegal stay abroad' - and so he arrived at the Czechoslovakian border asking to be let in. They chased him away. He had to legalize his relation with the republic first. He returned to Munich, took a plane to the US, and in Miami he jumped off a skyscraper…"

The judge came back to the table and sat down. He looked at the divorce application sheet without focusing on it. I saw that he had a film running in his head.

"Well, in the book, Tereza and Tomas, were able to get back with no problems, across the border, I mean."

"Yes, the first years were kind of unsettled. I know emigrants who had the nerves to return to get out their books or other precious things after the first panic stricken escape. Though once the Russian friendly collaborators were in full control, they let the curtain down in both directions."

"All this because of the Yalta agreement, right." said the judge sternly, "Many Americans were not in favor of it, me neither, expecting things to get tense. Stalin has never renounced the 'proletarian revolution'. And he took Yalta as a free pass to Central Europe. Both sides were afraid of each other, and the war against 'das Dritte Reich' was still raging. At that moment, I was already in Bavaria; February 45."

The judge now focused on the divorce sheet again. I hoped he would go on to tell me what he was doing there, in Bavaria, as a lawyer - was he involved in the Denazification? Was he at the Nürnberg Trials? I was curious but I didn't dare to ask. Already as a small boy, a "pioneer", I felt great respect for the Western allied soldiers. We were obliged to visit the Russian military cemetery in Prague every year on May 9, stood guard there and in the streets, but we had to ignore the part where the Allied soldiers laid buried. From time to time I went alone there and tried to decipher the inscriptions on the stones; all these places behind the Iron curtain: Next to the USA, the British, and the Canadian soldiers, are buried Pakistani, Indian, Australian, and New Zealand troopers.

Three

I am writing this in 2015. Around a million or so refugees have flocked into Europe in this one year alone; the failed Arab spring and the Civil war in Syria drove them out of their homes. Compared with their dramatic flight, mine might be considered a Sunday afternoon stroll. Shouldn't I stop? Is the number and the difficulty of a flight decisive for telling one's story? Does it have to be dramatic? Blood curdling? Dead bodies... I am ruminating about the difference between then and now; there is no difference in a human life in the beginning nor in death... In the end, I've decided not to hold back my story. It is my story. I only have this one unique story, just this one; I've managed to survive and to start a new life, speaking a new language (actually two), spending my life's end in a country which I didn't choose but was accepted into and given a chance. There was even the possibility of going home, going back there with my Swiss wife and children, to live there - for twelve years. Yes, I'm telling the story of my divorce in 1985, when I would have said "no, forget it" to anyone if I should be asked about an eventual disintegration of the Soviet system, about the end of the Russian oppression[1]

---

1 Kundera says: "All previous crimes of the Russian empire had been committed under the cover of a discreet shadow. The deportation of a million Lithuanians, the murder of hundreds of thousands of Poles, the liquidation of the Crimean Tatars remain in our memory... sooner or later they will therefore be proclaimed as fabrications."page 67

of so many nations.[2] And yet, it was this year, 1985, when Michail Gorbachev was elected General Secretary by the Politburo and had started the glasnost and perestroika which four years later brought the Berlin Wall down and a month later the Velvet Revolution in Prague, which brought Václav Havel up to the castle. On December 27, 1989, Havel was inaugurated as president of Czechoslovakia. Unbelievable! And then, on top of all these unexpected changes, a local rock musician, Michael Kocáb, a newly elected deputy of the assembly, negotiated and supervised the repatriation of the Russian troops, only a year and a half after Václav Havel became president. As of June 30, 1991, the occupation forces did withdraw completely from Czechoslovakia. To accomplish this, 925 transports were necessary to move 73,500 soldiers back to Russia together with 39,000 family members; 1,220 tanks and 2,500 other military vehicles; 105 aircrafts, 175 helicopters, and 95,000 tons of ammunition.

The crucial point, in my eyes now, is the question of whether the refugees of 2015 have some kind of hope that the situation will change and that they will be able to go home. Yes, unexpectedly I was able to go back after thirty years abroad, but twelve years later I realized I could not live there anymore. I didn't want to have my children grow up in that damaged society where people on every level had lost all ethics and morals, the political and social apparatus functioning according to the corrupt behavior code which, after the invasion and occupation of 1968, still circulated in the blood of three generations of twist-

---

2 Again, I'm writing this down in 2015, so add Syria, fourth year into the civil war. And Russia is present to help whom? The dictator who murders his own people.

ed backbones:[3] the one which suffered the shock of 1938, the Munich Treaty, followed by six years of the German occupation, the revived democratic tradition crushed by the Communist takeover only three years later in February 1948, and the last chance to regain decency, the Prague Spring, choked to death by the Russians in 1968. With my experience of life in working democratic systems, I couldn't take it anymore, the more because my opinion, my experience, wasn't met with any interest, to put it mildly; "We do it our way, buddy" was something I got to hear on many occasions. So, unfortunately the Communist party was not forbidden, and it was able to cultivate its destructive strategy in both chambers, causing continuous inefficiency in law making and the restitution process. Seeing ex Secret Police agents (STB) sitting in parliament, people of the same breed as Putin is, still having their privileges and means to mal-influence the society, was hard to take.

My father died in 1986. No satisfaction for him. I didn't get to see him. When the system unexpectedly changed, my mother used to say "... if Josef could open his eyes just for a few seconds. And see it!" When my mother died, in 2006, just having celebrated her 80th birthday, things sped up, nothing was holding us back anymore and in 2009 we took off for Switzerland again.

And it was me now, who was mumbling to himself "... it is better she does not know, does not see what has happened with all the regained freedom they waited for all their lives."

Again, I have to mention Milan Kundera. As with his

---

3 Kundera says: "... that cowardice was slowly but surely becoming the norm of behavior and would soon cease being taken for what it actually was." page 181

book *The Joke* where he writes about the Stalinist fifties and the loosening sixties, then about the Russian invasion in the *Unbearable Lightness of Being*, so with his novel *Ignorance* about the impossibility of a return; he touches the nerve of the basic human condition. All three books correspond with my confession here. I didn't investigate, I just had to go through with it, and I owe Mr. Kundera more than respect for his masterly fabulation of our twisted compatriot lives.

Four

"In 1968, the year of the Russian invasion - you were 19 years old, I see here," remarked the judge after quickly going over the one sheet divorce application. "How did you get out? Did you leave alone? With family? Why did you go?"

"Actually, I followed my girlfriend. She went ahead of me, together with her mother who decided to emigrate immediately, during the very first days of the invasion, and with good reason. My girlfriend didn't want to go and neither did I. We couldn't believe it - was it all over? We thought it must be some kind of misunderstanding. Later we imagined some kind of a resistance, we hoped for a withdrawal of the Russians... But day by day, facing the soldiers on every corner, facing the incredible number of armored vehicles and hearing the planes overhead, nonstop... We had our independent information, in short waves, the regional radios reported one after the other for ten minutes each. But within two weeks all hope was lost. Kundera writes that within a week we became a vassal of the Russians. Well yes, we were humiliated and violated, we were made a vassal by force. The only consolation might be that all this happened without any real bloodshed. No one returned the salves of the panic stricken Russian soldiers. And on top of the confused situation, the troops of the first occupation wave were exchanged for new ones, and they were told that the damage they saw around them was caused by the counterrevolution, the Czechs..."

"Conspiracy, diversification, the state beheaded... You people had to have good nerves there, I've got to say," commented the judge on my recapitulation. He knew what he meant by 'beheaded' - the government and the central bureau of the party were taken hostage and moved to Moscow to sign an agreement of consent, meaning they signed a capitulation.

"The question stood in the air: 'Are we cowards? Are we really giving in so easily?' There is an interesting coincidence regarding the word 'cowards': ten years before, in 1958, a book by Josef Škvorecký with the title *Cowards* was published. It was immediately forbidden and the whole edition destroyed.[1] I remember picking up this ambivalent feeling, this self-doubting, and I remember writing down a poem which went something like: 'Coward! Dice thrown at your feet, welted leaves, murdered minds. Though screaming at the mirror, your equal, I, there won't be ever peace in your life...'"

There was silence for a while. After that kind of personal ventilation, I had to collect myself. The judge also stayed silent for a while, he seemed to be touched.

"Why did we go? Not only because of the humiliation but because we were deprived of our dreams. You know, the prevailing energy inside of us, the young ones, was

---

1 ČSSR President Antonín Novotný and the KSČ Central Committee accused Škvorecký of "defamation of anti-fascist resistance and denigration of the Red Army", copies were withdrawn from sale and destroyed, and the author was dismissed from his post as editor of the magazine *Světová literatura* ("World Literature"). The novel survived and was republished in Czechoslovakia in 1964, 1966 and in the Prague Spring of 1968. When this ended in the Warsaw Pact invasion of Czechoslovakia, Škvorecký and his wife fled to Canada. *Cowards* was published in English by in the USA by Grove Press in 1970 and in Canada by Škvorecký's own 68 Publishers in 1972.

to explore the world, express our feelings, play music, go for a life not limited by any ideology, old or new one. And above all, we were certainly in opposition to a life with our heads bent down, a life on our knees."

"You said, your girlfriend's mother had a good reason to go immediately - what kind of reason?"

"She was a journalist. She was an editor with the literary weekly which published the Two Thousand Words Proclamation.[2] Imagine, a literary weekly with an edition of 300,000 by a population of 14 million... And all the journalists, like her, all the writers, were on a list the Russians tried to fetch as they detained the party members, the government, and the parliament leaders..."

"Yes, I remember, Kundera tells the story of the abduction. In his story, Dubcek speaks to the people, he stands for the state representatives, he is the symbol of the human face in socialism."

"He is, he does represent that. He is short of breath, Kundera tells us. And Dubcek's "au bout de souffle" becomes a simile for the state of shock people fell into, a simile for the state of mind of the whole society: being short of breath. Yet he was simplifying. Alexander Dubcek was only the first secretary of the Communist party. At home, I mean in Prague, we kept our skepticism about communists, 'human face' or not. He was drilled in Moscow, he learned Marxism-Leninism. He was naive, emotional; he

---

2 Many people don't realize that the so called "Prague Spring" or the "Socialism with Human Face" was not only about freedom of speech, freedom to travel, freedom to be free. It was also about the last chance to save the failing industry, the economy as such. After twenty years of socialist order, Czechoslovakia was losing its ground. And: "To sum up, the country reached a point where its spiritual health and character were both ruined." https://en.wikipedia.org/wiki/The_Two_Thousand_Words).

won people's heart… And there was the fact that he was of Slovak origin, like a few other main characters such as Gustav Husák and Vasil Bilak, the hardliners, the Moscow faithful comrades who then took over."

"And still are in power, yes. So Czechs don't like the Slovaks…"

"No, no, we get along and if not, then it's the other way around: they don't like us. They don't like their 'older brother', so to say."

The judge smiled at my comment but he came back to the situation in August: "I remember pictures on television of your people heading for the border, some on foot only, or on bicycles…"

"Well, the first two weeks it was possible to travel using any possible transportation, by car or by train or by plane, no one needed any passport, the Czech border guard and customs let people pass through. The Russians were not yet in control of the borders to Germany or Austria. But since I had hesitated on whether I would go as well, suddenly the information was passed on that you had to have a proper passport for the Western countries, and visas as well as transit visas… My girlfriend's mother - both my girlfriend and her mother had already gone - provided me with some contacts in Prague which might help in case the situation should worsen. The most useful one proved to be the one for the improvised visa office of Western Germany which was set a up in a hotel room at the hotel Jalta[3] on Wenceslas square. So, using all kinds of local contacts, I managed to get a passport and I faked an invitation letter

---

3 Nowadays the Cold War museum is inside, in the previously concealed nuclear fallout shelter from the 1950s; the military headquarters of the Warsaw Pact countries would have their base there.

to a wedding of my pen pal Sandra in London."

"What do you mean by 'faked'?"

We talked and it got even darker in the room. The judge did not make a move, he did not switch on the light. We talked. Hours went by, outside the lights of nightly San Francisco shown...

"Using my old typewriting machine, I wrote a letter to myself, the wedding invitation, and faked Sandra's signature. I took the envelope from the last letter she had sent me from London and folded the invitation inside. The next morning, I went to the British Embassy. After a while, I was let into a small office where the clearance officer stretched out his arm to see my papers: my freshly issued passport, the entry visa application, and the faked letter. He went through the papers, took the letter out of the envelope and glanced at it. I had the impression that he knew. He kind of suppressed an ironic smile and asked who Sandra was. I told him she was my old-time pen pal from the satiric magazine *Punch* and that we had been friends since 1965. Almost imperceptibly nodding, the official took a large visa-stamp and punched the visa onto a page of the passport. He handed it to me and said, 'Good luck to you!', looking straight into my eyes."

"Lucky you, forger", interjected the judge.

"Now, I still had to get the two transit visas, the German one and the Belgian one. I didn't have any means to buy an airline ticket so I intended to go by train. The day after that I went to the hotel Jalta where I approached a certain person at the reception and I was led up to the room where the Germans issued visas on the go. The day after that I spent in a waiting line at the Belgian embassy. The paper work was done. Now the train ticket. I just had money for the stretch to Frankfurt, one way. That was it. Farther steps had to be left up to fate. In Frankfurt, I knew there was a Swiss consulate, where I could apply for a visa to Switzerland, to join my girlfriend and her clan."

I stopped talking and looked up at the face of the judge. He was attentive, with a slight nod he urged me to go on with my story.

"What do you mean by 'her clan'?"

"The mother of my girlfriend and her relatives. During WWII, this woman was married to a Jewish man and at the end of the German occupation of April 1945 she helped him go into hiding in order not to be transported to Therezienstadt. Later they were divorced and in 1948 the man emigrated, right after the Communist turn over. He was a talented businessman and was already well established in Switzerland in the late fifties. Now, his ex-wife expected help while she was on the run in '68…"

"And?"

"He provided her and her relatives, 'the clan', with some financial means but did not offer a place to stay. So that's why I joined them in Bern, in a pension type of hotel - called Hospiz zu Heimat, meaning 'Hospice at Home'. What an irony…"

"That's for sure."

"Later on, we moved into a three-room apartment and I started to work at a telephone exchange in Bern to help out financially. My girlfriend started to study at the university. It was not easy for her mother to find a decent job."

"Now, let's go back. Tell me more about how you succeeded in overcoming the Iron Curtain…"

"Well, there is not much more to say. From my family and my relatives, I was fortunate to collect some western currencies, which was actually forbidden to keep; about five pounds, ten marks and about as many Swiss francs. They were all rolled together tightly. I put the money into an emptied soft cigarette box. The brand was the Egyptian *Golden West*, replacing the cigarettes afterwards. The next day I boarded a regular express train to Paris, departing at around 10 AM. I'll make it short: my mother saw me off, I leaned out of the train window, waving back to her for as long as I could see her.

It was like a 'Big Bang' to my generation, in the end. My close friends sooner or later emigrated to Toronto, to San Francisco, to Melbourne, to London, or to Frankfurt. Only one close friend stayed behind because he was drafted. We were a great bunch, we had nicknames... I was called 'dedek' which means something like 'grandad'. There was also Dr. Mundy, Ava, Flex, Boban... The girls - they were not nicknamed, strange... It is also strange that, except for one girl, I don't know what happened to them, though I'm in touch with the males. One reason might be that the women preferred to melt into their new societies, getting rid of the emigre aura. Kundera talks about this as not letting oneself be framed into the kitsch an emigrant's life might become..."

The judge chimed in, halting my wandering reflections and asking once again about my story. "So the train you boarded was going to Paris. And you got off in Frankfurt, I assume... But the crossing of the border to Germany, no trouble there?"

"If I remember correctly, I was sitting alone in the compartment, on the window seat, facing forward. Arriving at the boarder station, I saw Russian soldiers spread all along the platform, but when the train finally stopped, it was the

Czech border patrol that came in. Certainly I was nervous. I was nervous about the money in the cigarette pack which I placed in an ostentatious way on the little side table, I was nervous even more about the discrepancy between the British visa and the ticket which was valid only as far as Frankfurt. The patroller checked my papers wordlessly, and shortly two Russian soldiers appeared behind them. As soon as the border patrol sensed the Russians at their backs, they returned my passport together with all my other papers and nodded almost imperceptibly in sympathy, moving on to the next compartment. One of the Russian soldiers stepped into my compartment, looked above and under the benches, then he left, ignoring my presence completely. And that was it. After a while the train moved on and crossed the Yalta demarcation line, the Iron Curtain was lifted for me, on September 21, 1968.

The year 1968 was such a full year so far: I had successfully graduated from the special college for telecommunication, I was admitted to the Charles University to study journalism, and - I fell in love. Also, in the spring I started to shoot my first film, together with a group of friends from different parts of Prague. We were a clique of girls and boys, I told you already, practically all of the same age, who usually met at the pub U Vejvodů in the Old Town of Prague. It was such a beautiful spring, everyone excited, coming and going from a meeting to a meeting, from a meeting to a music concert, from a concert to a movie theatre; there was the Czech Wave on, the films from Italy and France and one from the USA which awakened my desire to make such films myself: *The Savage Eye*. It was a craze of things happening one after the other. There were sparks set off every day if not every hour. Nowadays I wonder how many hours I slept - four? Five? I remember falling down on my face, sleeping sometimes during the day only to get up twenty minutes later to set off to another event. Since I was publishing the college magazine, I had access to all the meetings where the Prague spring was forged: those of the Writers' or Film Makers' Unions, even those on the party level. As a student journalist, I was present in Vladislav's Hall when the Communist president Novotny was dismissed and general Svoboda was elected (he was not a party member but he followed its orders. You might know about him). I was sitting on the sill of one of the Gothic windows there, looking down on the aged party members, now following bravely the order of the day. My feelings? Great satisfaction! And promise...

For me, on the political level, it started on January 5, that year. I fetched the newspaper, as I did every day, before jumping on a street car. Once aboard I started to read Dubcek's speech. I lifted my eyes from the article on the front page, incredulous of its content. I was not the only one stunned. Other people in the street car were lifting their heads from the newspapers, looking around, wondering if this might really be true, our eyes meeting fleetingly. And in those eyes, there was this 'spark of promise'.

In the craze that followed, I soon ran out of financial means (I never had any money from my parents) and I started to look around for a job. Finally, together with a friend, I set off to GDR where I had already worked the year before: It was a job on a construction site associated with the building of the iron works of Eisenhüttenstadt, near Frankfurt upon Oder, right at the Polish border. And that was where I experienced the beginning of the occupation during the night of August 20 to August 21. I have to add that two days before that I was involved in a discussion about the forces and motives behind the Prague Spring, and the German head of our work group apparently did not like what I had to say about it. So the morning after I was summoned to the canteen, and there I got to know the chief of the party committee on the construction site. To my astonishment, it happened to be the cleaning lady from the canteen. Nevertheless, I was strongly reprimanded and in the end I was sentenced to an unconditional deportation back to Czechoslovakia within 24 hours, as my young age and my 'decent behavior so far' were considered an extenuating circumstance. What did I do? I was explaining to my German work colleagues that people back in Czechoslovakia were already collecting gold among themselves to strengthen the currency, the Czech crowns. To illustrate the weakness of the socialist currency, I put my hand into the pocket of my jeans and showed them a handful of the local aluminum coins then in use, mocking its tin-metal quality: 'just toy money'.

My deportation could not be executed because the next day we were all summoned to the canteen where a higher-ranking man from the party regional committee read to us an article published in *Neues Deutschland*, awkwardly translated by some 'Sudetendeutsche' explaining the move to occupy Czechoslovakia by the Warsaw Pact armies. We already knew. Right after we started to work on the site - we used to start at 5 in the morning - one other Czech student who used to listen to a small transistor radio all the time, run up to us screaming on the edge of insanity 'You idiots, the Russians are in Prague!'. And almost immediately we heard the sound of airplanes flying in high altitude above us. Those were now the troops brought continuously into our country from the Soviet military bases in Poland.

So after a moment listening at the canteen to the Ulbricht's propaganda, we started to drum on the tables to suppress the apparent lies we could not stand being read to us. Everything was propaganda, every word was signaling the communist paranoia. In the end, we were mass deported to our housing where we had to stay and wait for further instructions. Back in our quarters, we immediately tuned into the Czech short wave transmitters and followed the news. The news was bad.

Unfortunately, it didn't take long and some officials accompanied by the Vopo, the Volkspolizei, came in and confiscated all our transistor radios. But about an hour later, a courageous German coworker snuck in and brought us a transistor radio of his own so we were able to stay up to date.

The following day we were herded into buses, collecting other Czechs along the road to Berlin and from there the convoy of buses drove to Dresden. The buses came to a halt at the freight station where there was a special train ready to bring us back to Czechoslovakia.

Soon the train was full and started to move out of Dresden and along the river Elbe toward the border. People exchanged information. There were new acquaintances to be made, some people were worried about when we were going to arrive in Prague, and whether they would make it to the other railroad station in order to reach their train connections farther on; there was apparently martial law beginning at 10 PM... Then past Bad Schandau the train entered the narrow passage and we spotted huge Czechoslovakian flags fixed on the rocks right past the border.

Suddenly it was quiet. Then everybody on the train started to sing the national anthem *Kde domov můj*, which means 'Where is my home?'; many had tears in their eyes.

The last two things I remember of the home coming is the scene in our compartment after dark. My friend Flex was sitting opposite me. In his arms slept an unknown fragile girl with her head on his shoulder. I envied him. Then we got to Prague, it was already past 10 PM, so covered by the night we moved along the houses to reach our homes.

Five

Instead of trying to recollect what I'd told judge O'Donnell about my impression of *The Unbearable Lightness of Being* (30 years ago), let me make use of an artistic license and beam myself to the present time, the year 2015, to leaf through my diary and quote here my authentic impression after having finished the book sometime between 1984 and 1985:

> *This book is the key novel for the '68 generation, and similarly for all other affected generations. Though not pronounced up front, it expresses the longing for an end for all those who are consequent in their moral stand points; that's why Tereza and Tomas have to die in an accident, enwrapped by a deadly melancholy caused by the country's tragic end, the invasion of Russian troops in August '68. It is a report written with discouraging worldly sobriety. It sketches the only possible love of those who are bound together, maybe even brought together by a chance, but certainly both in dire straits, quietly enduring their fate, not capable of living outside of their occupied home country. Pondering the characters of the book, their fate, and the life here, within the local, western civilization has a bitter aftertaste, the life of an emigre is devoid of soul...*

Let me add that when I have left Prague in September of 1968, and joined my girlfriend in Bern, we went through exactly such a "deadly melancholia" for about half a year. My girlfriend suffered greatly and often cried in hysteria.

She would have preferred to return, as Tereza did. Only because of me and because of her mother, whom she felt obligated to follow and stay with, did she refuse to go back. And I was certainly no Tomas, no physician with a possible career to make in the West. I was a 19-year-old nobody (though like Tomas I liked to look at attractive women). But in spite of our melancholia and homesickness, we taught ourselves German, we started to work respectively, to study, we learned to live with less sensuality, our Slavonic nativeness subdued. We separated a year later though, and mixed with the Swiss, and that was the best remedy, the best way out of desperation over our fate. And by and by the certain normality of our everyday life had subdued 'the lightness of being' as well.

Kundera writes that the characters in his book just represent possibilities of a life, that it is not his confession, but that it is an investigation into human life in our time. In my lines here, you have gotten a confession which needed almost fifty years to develop and ripen. Writing this confession was caused by the empathy of judge O' Donnell, the synchronicity of having read Kundera's book at the same time as him, right after it was published for the first time in 1984, and the coincidence of his military career in Central Europe at the end of WWII; and by my urge to save a trace of this one refugee life, mine, unique as any other life of any other refugee.

Now, in 2015, even more than in 1985, I am aware of the novel's philosophical value on the base of an individual search for a decent life. Not a mission of any kind, but life: truthful, authentic, and free of kitsch.[1] And actually,

---

1 "Missions are stupid, Tereza. I have no mission. No one has. And it's a terrific relief to realize you're free, free of all missions."

I finally dare to say that I understand the title... I've the impression that the film has laid a somewhat misleading track to its understanding, and most people remember *The Unbearable Lightness of Being* as a private drama, full of promiscuity and sex (By the way, in those times you made love, you were not having sex.). On top of that, the film ends up in kitsch,[2] the worst sin one might commit in the eyes of the author of the novel.

---

2 "... a new utopia, a paradise: a world where a man is excited by seeing a swallow and Tomas can love Tereza without being disturbed by the aggressive stupidity of sex." page 237

Six

In the end the judge shuffled the divorce papers: "So, let's have look... But again, it's your wife who is filing for divorce! I cannot do anything. Be here Monday morning, eight sharp, with her to sign. The office to do it in will be 13B."

I leaned back and watched the judge stand up. In the twilight, I looked at the window and the city of San Francisco behind it. I glanced along the walls full of books, taking in the impression that a person of authority had taken the time to listen, was competent to understand (no kitsch asked for but maybe told) and whom I instinctively trusted. He passed the papers to me while I was standing up. "Let's go", he said, "and let me thank you for the time we spent together. God bless you."

The judge locked the door to his office, and together we walked the corridor to the central staircase. We didn't talk anymore; an eerie silence was all around us, penetrated only by the echo of our steps.

Having left the City Hall building, I still had many, many thoughts racing in my head. I was thinking over what I had told Mr. O'Donnell, and what I had forgotten or not mentioned, and what I should have told him...

The confession was not complete and I felt frustrated. I rushed home - I mean hurried to my wife's place - where I hoped to find her at home and stay with her for another 48 hours plus - and then to take off for ever.

Seven

Once again 2015. I find myself in a provincial town of Switzerland, in the so called "City of the Ambassador". I'm divorced, living in a one room apartment, with too much time to occupy myself with myself. The children are on their own; now I understand my mother when she lost her son. Sometimes I talk to myself. "When you talk to yourself, you're not alone anymore," Herta Müller said. These lines are the result of such a state of mind. I wish to keep talking, I have the urge. I am talking to you, to my companions from Prague, and to some people from other countries I passed through as well. I find moral support in the ongoing work of writers like Julian Barnes, Richard Ford, Martin Amis, Paul Auster, and Haruki Murakami - we are all about the same age. Haruki Murakami is the one born in 1949, the same year as I. What I cannot fabulate by myself I find in the works of these masters, and in the works yet by other men and women of letters. Haruki Murakami sums it up: "I was born in 1949, entered high school in 1961 and the university in 1967. ... So there I was, during the most vulnerable, most immature, and yet most precious period of life, breathing in everything about this live-for-the-moment decade, high on the wildness of it all..." - thus starts Haruki Murakami's short story *A Folklore For My Generation: A Prehistory Of Late-Stage Capitalism.*[1] He goes on: "I'm not boasting about the times I lived through. I'm

---

1 in *Blind Willow, Sleeping Women*, 2005.

simply trying to convey what it felt like to live through that age, and the fact that there really was something special about it. Yet if I were to try to unpack those times and point out something in particular that was exceptional, I don't know if I could. What I'd come up with if I did such a dissection would be these: the momentum and the energy of the times, the tremendous spark of promise." ...Here it is: "*the tremendous spark of promise*". Well, in 2015 I don't see any "spark of promise". Rather I see much doubt and self-deconstruction. We're even failing to defend our identity. My gratitude to and my admiration of men like judge John B. O'Donnell are all the more stronger.

What has happened in those years gone by? In Kundera's land the two nations have separated, thank God peacefully, and now the Czechs and the Slovaks are independent and govern themselves on their own responsibility. The expatriates stayed mostly in their new countries, not being welcomed back home, their rich experience disregarded or even mocked. A few did what I've done, have taken the ashes of their ancestors and spread them in one spot, the family graveyards liquidated.

Eight

I am unwinding these thoughts on an immediate impulse: today in the morning when I read the message Jennifer was gone – with some of you around her – I had to go out into the courtyard and there was a bird chirping in the branches of our central tree. The bird kept dancing in the air above. Here, I never heard a bird like that before. The bird, similar to a blue tit, to a blue cap maybe, was chirping away in the still barren crown of the catalpa tree - right there, where I had sat down with Jennifer not quite a year ago. There, we were at peace with the world, with each other, for a good while.

Jennifer was a friend to me through the worst. She was a messenger of freedom and love to Prague in the seventies. Jennifer was someone I have sensed at my side all the time since we met in February 1974: a straight, beautiful, open hearted person. I owe her so much...

She was someone who would prefer - and would have deserved - to live in a Russian fairy tale. But instead she had to struggle through life until the very end, leaving too soon...

Good Bye to her.

Nine

It was in February 2013, ten years after my wife's death, that I was able to visit the Bay Area for the last time and that my wife's sister surprised me with a little box, neatly wrapped up, saying: "I knew you would come by one day. I saved half of her ashes so that you may spread them around where she wished, where the other half is since 2003. Inside the box, there are also ashes from her beloved tomcat..." So, the next day I excused myself from my friends and drove down to Crissy Fields to fulfill her last wish. Again, in the afternoon I had to leave for Europe; the departures from San Francisco always on a tight schedule: like after the marriage, like after the divorce, like now, after the last "Good bye" to my life long companion.

At this point, the one moment comes to my mind again and again: When Jennifer brought me to the Oakland airport, after two years of life together and freshly wed, knowing she might not see me ever again. I stepped out of the car, yet I was held on the spot, I stayed waiting on the sidewalk where she drove off, and for sure, in a minute or two she passed by again, not stopping but saying in this way yet another 'good bye'. 'An unbearable heaviness' fell on me, the heaviness of my decision to make a step back, to get in the reverse gear for the first time in my life, to leave Jennifer, to leave my dreamed of California.

About The Author

Georg Aeberhard was born on February 25, 1949 in Prague, Czechoslovakia. He attended the College of Telecommunication and following the Russian invasion of Czechoslovakia in 1968, emigrated to Switzerland. He has worked in lighting, production management, and script writing for CONDOR FILM Ltd. in Zürich. He has also done freelance work as a theatre directing assistant in Bern and Zürich. In the 1970s, he earned a BA in arts and film from San Francisco State University, USA. Georg speaks Czech, German, English, Italian, French, Spanish, and Russian. He is also both a Swiss and Czech citizen and has two children.

Information and Sources

All Milan Kundera's quotes derive from the first edition of his book *The Unbearable Lightness of Being*, HARPER & ROW, PUBLISHERS, New York, 1984

The images in this book illustrate the text below, above, or next to which they appear.

They are of much lower resolution than the original (copies made from these images would be of very inferior quality).

The use of the images in this book do not limit the copyright owner's rights to market or sell the work in any way.

The images in this book are used on various websites, so their use in this book does not make them significantly more accessible or visible than they already are.

The images in this book are being used in an informative way and should not detract from the original works.

No free or public domain images have been located for these images.

Made in the USA
Lexington, KY
22 July 2017